AF247534

© Fitway Publishing 2007
Original Editions in French and in English
English language translation by Christie Tam

All rights reserved. No part of this book may be reproduced in any form
without the prior written permission of the publisher

Design: Garnas Design
Production: Patty Holden

ISBN: 978-2-7528-0264-4

Printed in China

www. fitwaypublishing.com
Fitway Publishing is an imprint of Silverback Books, Inc.
55 New Montgomery Street, Suite 500
San Francisco, CA 94105
USA

Fight

philippe di folco

contents

MONTANA®
MONTANA
BOXI
SPO
MMB 100
12oz

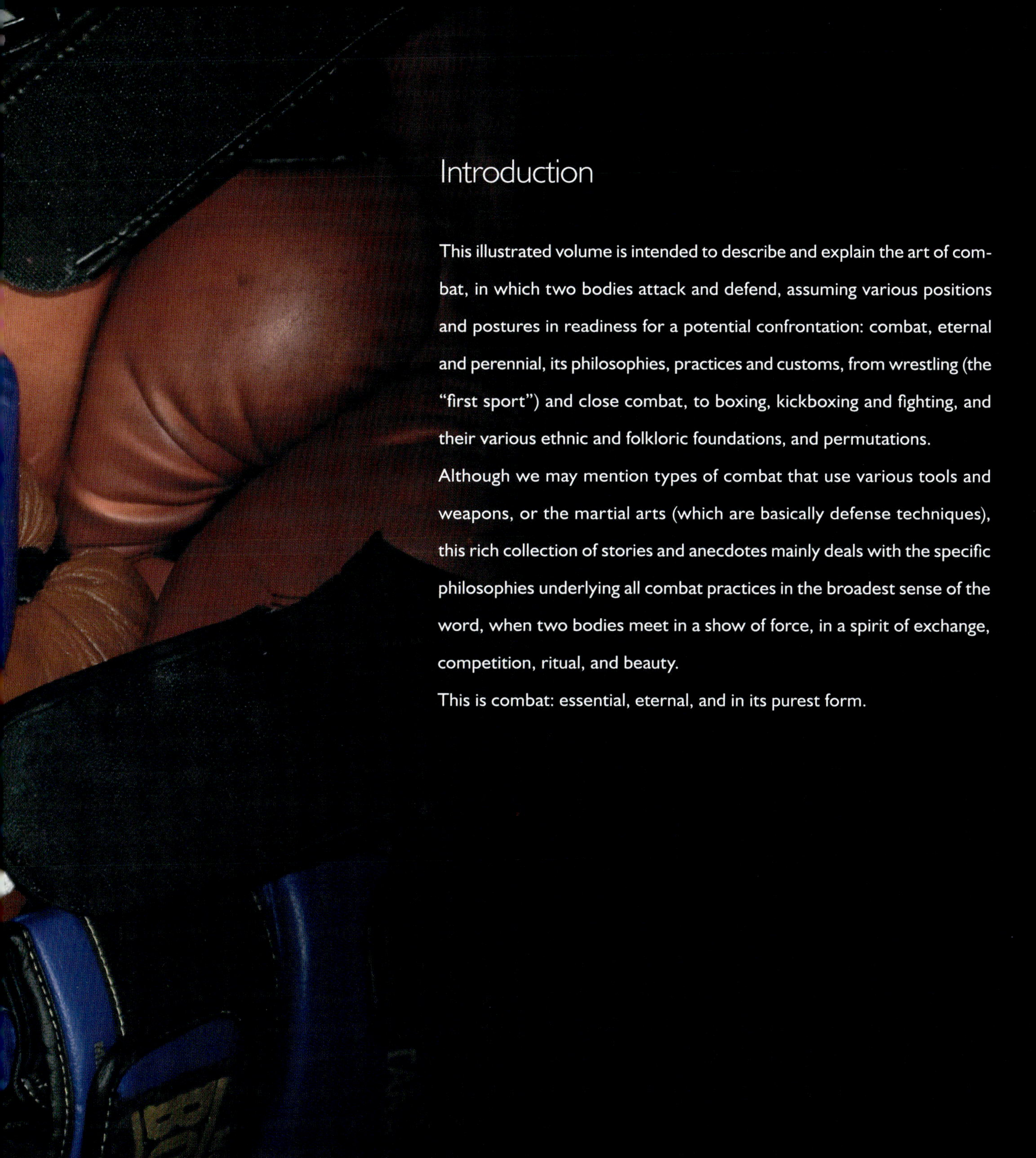

Introduction

This illustrated volume is intended to describe and explain the art of combat, in which two bodies attack and defend, assuming various positions and postures in readiness for a potential confrontation: combat, eternal and perennial, its philosophies, practices and customs, from wrestling (the "first sport") and close combat, to boxing, kickboxing and fighting, and their various ethnic and folkloric foundations, and permutations.

Although we may mention types of combat that use various tools and weapons, or the martial arts (which are basically defense techniques), this rich collection of stories and anecdotes mainly deals with the specific philosophies underlying all combat practices in the broadest sense of the word, when two bodies meet in a show of force, in a spirit of exchange, competition, ritual, and beauty.

This is combat: essential, eternal, and in its purest form.

The Origins of Combat

Part One:
The Origins
of Combat

Although combat, both close (wrestling) and apart (boxing), is closely regulated today, there was certainly a time when it was natural and free, bare-handed, between two people of the same gender. Combat is one of the first sports practiced in every civilization. Every ethnic group in the world has developed one or more unique forms of single combat. Even today, highly industrialized societies are still drawn to such forms of combat that combine ancient, ethnic rituals with the desire to let loose, as reflected in the growing number of clubs and the appearance of numerous treatments of the subject (films, matches, video games, etc.).

It appears that human beings have always been infatuated with this sort of combat, not unlike "young animals who test their mettle all day long with claws and teeth," according to Charles Ardant du Picq (1821–1870), one of the first essayists to turn his attention to the subject. Wherever we look—not counting childhood and adolescence when such battles seem to go with the territory—we discover obvious signs of humankind's real fascination with hand-to-hand. Although the stakes vary (territory, food, sexual dominance), the goal is always the same: power. We've all seen the magnificent introduction to *2001, a Space Odyssey* (Stanley Kubrick, 1968). Even before weapons were invented, fists (and the muscles for grasping and crawling in general) were for a long time the only means of demonstrating strength and thereby expressing the will to dominate. At the heart of every human community is a "social order," which naturally leads to "transgression" of the established order or its opposite. Humanity

Egyptian Wrestlers, 1500 B.C.

never stops (re)inventing this order by challenging it in the context of a game or gamble. Through combat and victory, the bare-fisted individual achieves recognition, exclusiveness, and a sort of dignity that is more spiritual than physical. In most cases, this involves an event within a very precise framework: the ring, surrounded by witnesses and spectators. It's a rite of passage, a sacred ceremony, a simple sporting event, a voluntary or provoked chance to let off steam, a fight without weapons, or martial techniques. It's two bodies, barely clothed, face-to-face, wanting to measure themselves against one another, following pre-established rules, with death as the only taboo.

Primitive peoples and art of physical games

Although human history, art and literature, and the evolution of psychological thought support the popular notion that rough play is bad, this is largely contradicted by the passion all cultures have demonstrated for the game of fighting. It's also true that something that starts out as a mere game can sometimes take a tragic turn, resulting in extreme pain, loss of a vital organ, and bloodshed, if not loss of life, which contradicts our noble, joyous, and festive image of ancient single combat. So why should the word "rough" (meaning coarse and unsophisticated) be inconsistent with the more civilized ideal that we try to impose on human relations, when it is combat that allows a person to escape his lot, make a name for himself, and find redemption?

Gilgamsh & Enkidu, Sumerian Mythology
2000 B.C.

The Bible starts out with the story of the mortal struggle between Cain and Abel, the primal combat, if there ever was one. Another example is the oldest known myth, The *Epic of Gilgamesh* (3000 B.C.), a quest for immortality and an education in the human condition. Although it portrays many bare-fisted fights with animals and gods, it begins with the confrontation between Gilgamesh, a hero without lineage, and Enkidu, "shaggy with hair" and with " a full head of hair like a woman," who was sent by the gods to replace him. Gilgamesh and Enkidu become friends. Various Western scholars have shown that epics such as the *Iliad* signaled the end of the matriarchy in our societies and the beginning of the reign of masculinity, suited to directing the first governments, and the first wars, as well as introducing an approach to humanity in all its complexity, the interplay between strength and weakness, where a hero weeps for his fate or a lost friend, and then triumphs, while also regretting having spilled the blood of his enemy. Gilgamesh, Achilles, and others also have feminine traits. The results of combat are ambiguous, and victory brings with it awful dilemmas!

According to the French scholar Serge Hutin (1927–1997), initiation is always a "process of passing from one supposedly inferior psychological state to a superior one." This may be true, but such rites of passage are part of what might be called the "playful instinct." Traces of this animal-like instinct can be found in ancient India, Pharonic Egypt, and the ancient Greco-Roman world. Nevertheless, in 1920, Pierre de Coubertin, the man who revived the Olympic Games, stated that "even when we impose conventional rules, the game between human beings doesn't automatically become sport. It's still just entertainment. To go beyond that, there must first be an athletic education." This is why "bare-chested" fighting outside established institutions has always had a bad reputation, or is practiced with a bad conscience.

Myths contain many single combats. One of the oldest wrestling matches was a fight between Hercules and Antaeus, king of Libya and son of Poseidon and Earth. Antaeus used to force strangers to wrestle with him, overcome them, and kill them. Every time he touched the earth, his strength was renewed. The two combatants prepared for battle. Both removed their lion skins, but whereas Hercules rubbed his body with oil Olympic-style, Antaeus poured hot sand onto his limbs, fearing that his contact with the earth through the soles of his feet would not be sufficient. Hercules had decided to husband his strength until Antaeus tired, but saw that "when he touched earth, so it was that he waxed stronger, wherefore some said that he was a son of Earth." Consequently, "Hercules hugged him, lifted him aloft, broke, and killed him." (Apollodorus, II, 5, 11). Through such myths we learn that Olympism, which originated in Greece in the eighth century B.C., gave us the first rules of combat, making it a veritable art that is still practiced today. Myths also contain stories of single combats using the feet and other parts of the body in addition to fists. Since the human body is capable of many tricks and turns, it wasn't

Children exercising fist fighting. 300 A.D. Marble sarcophagus (Louvre, Paris)

long before rules and restrictions were imposed to preserve life in all its sacredness. With the dawn of the age of humanism, another golden rule was added: do no harm or limit suffering.

The original combat arena

Ancient combat required a number of basic elements:

- A reason: a challenge, seasonal ritual, war, etc.
- Two adversaries face-to-face, stripped, and unarmed
- An area of confrontation (circle, square, rectangle)
- Lighting
- Spectators and
- A referee

An area of combat implies that one can be "outside" and "inside," not just in terms of physical space, but also in terms of the body. To leave the game of combat, one must quit, be wounded, reach one's pain threshold, or die. An "open" match is one in which all moves are allowed and a fatal outcome is expected. A "closed" match, on the other hand, involves precisely defined and assimilated rules for preventing fatal outcomes. Besides fighting with all parts of his body, the combatant can also employ his voice (cries and growls) to frighten his opponent. His skin can also be used for inscribing and identifying marks with symbolic meaning (drawings, tattoos, piercings, etc). Generally speaking, however, jewelry and finery are absent (to prevent an easy or dangerous hold). The reason matches often pass into legend is because they serve to commemorate the spirit, identify a part of manly youth, embody a public or private ethic—in other words, help a society learn the limits of living together. Thus, people don't fight just any old way in any old location. For example, the ancient Olympic Games that centered on single combat served as a sociopolitical outlet as of the eighth century B.C., and would make a comeback in the earlier twentieth century, this time on an international level.

The human body as a natural weapon

It doesn't take a degree in anatomy to know that every human body has its vital points and sensitive points. The entire human body could be seen as one sensitive point, since it's traversed by a network of nerve endings by means of which our brain records every contact, whether we're aware of it or not. Knowledge of the body allows a person to fight better while avoiding tragic, irreversible, or even fatal outcomes.

The body has about 50 vital and sensitive points. Acupuncturists know them all, of course, but so do athletic trainers. We instinctively protect the groin area and genitals (sensitive), but have a tendency to forget the throat and nape of the neck (vital), the heel, and the elbow (sensitive). Women also need to protect their chest.

The human body has three types of natural weapon:

■ Upper extremities: the hand is more effective when balled in a fist (boxing), but an open hand can be used for holds (wrestling); when slightly

"Jakob and the Angel" 1861 wall painting
by EugeDelaccroix, Saint-Sulpice Church, Paris

"Boxers" Knossos Palace, Crete, 1400 B.C.
Fresco Painting, Museum of Athens, Greece

open in a claw shape, the hand can be closed around a throat or jammed into the eyes; the forearm and biceps can be brought together in a hook (wrestling); an elbow jabbed in the stomach can be fatal; a single index finger in the eye can stop an adversary.

- Lower extremities: the knee, of course, kicking with the foot or both feet, hooks using the legs or thighs (freestyle wrestling).
- Head: it not only thinks (ducking, anticipating, etc.), but can also can be used to administer blows from the front (forehead) or the back; even the chin can be a weapon.

It's clear that all these moves involve risk to self and to the opponent. That's why there are rules. True freestyle wrestling (such as when someone attacks you with bare hands) can result in the immediate death of one or both parties. This dizzying prospect of a possible fatality is what has made combat so fascinating.

Greco-Roman wrestling

The society described in the *Iliad* (1200 B.C.) was already extremely athletic, with wrestling matches, foot races, and javelin throwing contests, all of which were serious competitions for trained contestants and steeped in religious ceremony. This was the birthplace of the religion of athletics, soon to develop its own brand of ceremonies and temples for daily worship. The ceremonies would be called *Games*: Pythian Games,

Isthmian Games, Nemean Games and, the most illustrious of all, the Olympic Games. The temples would be called *gymnasiums* (from *gumnos*, meaning "naked") and would become centers of municipal life where adolescents, adults, and old men gathered to worship the human body, which is the basis for all Hellenism. After the Romans conquered Greece in 144 B.C., they revived these practices within the framework of immense public baths (there were 10 in Rome in around 250 A.D.), where all types of men and women used numerous palestras (Roman gymnasiums, from [*palaio*], meaning "to wrestle") for practicing various forms of combat. Wrestling was a lot like it is today: wrestling from a standing position, where one of two contestants must lose his footing or be brought to his knees three times in order to be declared the loser, and wrestling on the ground, which had more in common with our own freestyle wrestling than with Greco-Roman, and often continued until the losing party begged for mercy. Such wrestling was also one of a series of complementary events (see below).

Pugilism was a type of primitive English boxing with the fists bare or perhaps wrapped in a cushioning material, although this is unclear. The Iliad describes a boxing match at the famous funeral games in honor of Patroclus, a friend of Achilles. Another more detailed story is found in Vergil's *Aeneid* (Book V). It describes a number of moves used in boxing today, including bobbing. The Latin poet uses the word *complector*,

"Boxer resting" Bronze statuer 100 B.C., National Museum, Rome

"Fighters", 450 B.C., Vase, Louvre, Paris

which has two meanings: a clinch between contestants and the embrace of lovers.

The question of the *caestus*, or ancient boxing glove, is more controversial. The caestus was a heavy leather strap reinforced with lead and wrapped around the fist and forearm that would not only have rendered the matches bloodier, but also more deadly. Such matches were rather rare, as were the *prize fights* in nineteenth-century England. We should just note that when a fist was thus weighted down, it could no longer be used for rapid jabbing. The game must have been more of an attempt to strike the opponent with a club-like blow that was slow and, therefore, easier to dodge, but obviously terrible if it found its mark.

There was also *pankration*, a combination of wrestling and boxing that also allowed kicking, probably as a means of keeping the opponent at a distance, as in modern French boxing. The Greeks also had the punching bag, which was a large ball (*korykos*) filled with grain or sand, depending on the strength of the one using it for training or exercise. Reintroduced in the nineteenth century, pankration has also been practiced in Corsica since its colonization by Greece.

Pankration was (and is again) an exhausting combination of boxing and wrestling. Punches were allowed, although contestants didn't wrap their hands. As with boxing and wrestling, this sport was divided into separate contests for adults and adolescents. Pankration first appeared in 648 B.C. at Olympia, where the first Olympic Champion of Pankration,

Lygdamus, first made an appearance, but it seems to have already existed by the Trojan War (Second Millennium B.C.). Pankration may have its origins in the Mycenaean, Ionian, Minoan, or even Egyptian civilization (2600 B.C.), since we know that one of the Egyptian wrestling styles was strangely similar to Greek Pankration. The name "pankration" is made up of the two Greek words "pan," meaning "all," and "kratos," meaning "strength." This could be interpreted as either "all strengths permitted" or "omnipotence," because weight classes had not yet been invented, and the most important thing was good technique. There were two types of pankration: *kato pankration*, which allowed continuing a fight on the ground, and *ano pankration*, which did not. The latter was used more often in preliminary competitions and resembled modern kickboxing. The contestants were supposed to strike one another for as long as they both remained standing. On the other hand, fighting on the ground turned into a fierce hand-to-hand wrestling match in which the two combatants rolled around on the sand or mud, grabbing, and wrapping themselves around one another while continuing to strike one another violently, each doing his utmost to render the other helpless, and extract an admission of defeat. Although popular, the art of pankration was wrapped in secrecy; each school and each family possessing this knowledge did its best to guard it, and were so successful that it disappeared altogether from the countries where it originated. The extreme violence of pankration, which permitted anything but eye and nose gouging, biting, carrying a weapon,

"The Combat of Naked Man" by Antonio Pollaiuolo, 1490 Louvre, Paris Edmond de Rothschild Collection.

or covering the hands with gauntlets, made this Olympic discipline the most dangerous of contests, sometimes resulting in the death of one of the fighters. Some philosophers, including Plato, criticized pankration, calling it brutal and unaesthetic. They thought the interests of the Greek nation would be better served by training warriors. It was "pankration versus the sword."

One of the most famous tales of pankration involves Creugas and Damoxenos, whose statues now stand in the Vatican. The story goes that if neither emerged victorious by sunset, the match would be halted, as was the rule. The law of *climax* was then applied, where each fighter was permitted by turns to strike his opponent, while the latter was not allowed to dodge the blow (similar to a penalty shot in soccer). The attacker was supposed to tell his opponent what position to take before striking him. After drawing lots, Creugas was allowed to strike the first blow. Asking Damoxenos to keep his arms at his sides, he gave him a powerful blow to the face. Damoxenos took it without moving. He then asked Creugas to raise his left arm, after which he proceeded to insert his fingers under his ribcage, and pull out his intestines!

Another story relates how Arrichion of Phigaleia was killed, but still won the match. He was caught in a choke hold and while trying desperately to free himself, he managed to seize his opponent's foot (some say toe) and twist it until he dislocated his ankle. Unable to stand the pain, his adversary raised his hand as a sign of defeat, at the same moment that the strangled Arrichion took his last breath. Arrichion was proclaimed the posthumous victor. The Agonothetes crowned his corpse and the scene was commemorated in a painting described by Philostratos.

Legend has it that although the Spartiates wrestled, they refused to participate in pugilism or pankration because of the practice of raising a finger to withdraw from a match—Spartiates could never admit defeat. Observers from that era also wrote of their pleasure at seeing girls and boys wrestling together in a gymnasium in Chios. In Sparta, it was not uncommon to attend public matches where young women willingly and unhesitatingly pitted themselves against the men.

Middle Ages and Renaissance

One of the most striking aspects of Western Christianity was its partial suppression of single combat sports—due, no doubt, to a fear of the body and the instincts aroused, even under controlled circumstances. The advent of the Order of Chivalry brought with it the notion of the duel. Once again, young men could distinguish themselves by fighting, though this time it was with arms. The Order was linked to the military regime, but there were also courtesan duels. The seigniorial and royal courts fostered verbal, polemical, and flirtatious jousting that was often poetic, giving rise to an entire literature (Provençal, among others), including the modern novel, and recycling ancient narratives with songs of illustrious battles. In the Middle East, the *Thousand and One Nights* relates numerous

"Hercules and Ante" Brass Sculpture by
Pier Giacomo Alari Bonacolsi, 1519

*"Fighters, Hercules and Cacus" print by
Michelangelo, 1534, Louvre, Paris*

battles between humans and genies, but only Persia has handed down a rich iconography, since Islam strictly forbids anthropomorphic representations. Beginning in the fourteenth century, artists of the Renaissance would exploit this material and portray battles between gods and goddesses, despite the prohibitions of the Church.

Also in the fourteenth century, persons calling themselves "masters of the noble science of defense" appeared in England. These men taught fighting techniques to civilians and soldiers. Their favorite disciplines were fencing with broadswords and rapiers, parrying with shields, and fist fighting. One of the later masters was none other than James Figg (1695–1734), boxing's first recognized champion who attracted the attention of the London society. The subsequent craze was the beginning of boxing as a sport.

The Far East: A philosophy of self-defense

The martial arts, which became tremendously popular in the West after its introduction in the twentieth century, are also worth mentioning. The philosophy behind a martial art promotes the personal development of its devotees for the very specific purpose of preparing them to meet any form of physical or mental aggression. We generally think of the Chinese, Indian, and Japanese cultures as favoring mass movements, rather than individual development, but the opposite is actually true. In the sixth century B.C., when the first defensive weapons made from hard metals (sabers, knives, and armor) arrived in Asia, the martial arts also appeared at a time of great political upheaval in China. Their teachings began to be set down in written form in the third century A.D. Confucius (551–479 B.C.), a contemporary of Lao-Tzu and Buddha, did not consider combat to be a major art, but he did recognize the "martial attitude" as one of the elements necessary for physical and mental equilibrium, though insufficient in itself. The solitary followers of an ancestral martial art can be compared to the figure of the European knight who is alone in his quest for grace. The martial arts are based on a Buddhist mysticism that resembles the Christian mysticism of the European knight.

There's a legend of an Indian monk named Bodhidharma who appeared one day at the Shaolin Temple at the foot of the Song Shan mountains in the Chinese kingdom of Wei. This monk taught a new, more direct form of Buddhism in which the disciples reached enlightenment through perpetual meditation. Bodhidharma himself sat for nine years contemplating the back of a cave before he began training other monks in his school. To help endure long hours of meditation, Bodhidharma taught breathing techniques and exercises to help those persevere, and better defend themselves in the remote mountains where they lived. These exercises were the basis for the martial art known as *Shaolin ch'uan-fa* or the "Way of the Shaolin Fist," and many other Chinese and Japanese martial arts have emerged from the same tradition. However, martial

" Tongan Boxers," 1840, Etching

arts were flourishing in India and China long before the mythical voyage of Bodhidharma.

Oddly enough, France has a discipline with basic techniques very similar to those of Asian martial arts. Commonly known as "savate" or "chausson," this discipline was perfected in the nineteenth century and went on to become what we now call, French boxing (la boxe francaise). It apparently emerged from a popular form of fighting that allowed punches, kicks, and wrestling holds. The techniques resemble those of karate. Despite the similarities, however, French boxing is not intended to be anything other than a recreational sport and means of self-defense, without any pretensions of offering a "path" or "way of life."

But the martial arts weren't the only philosophy of combat to come out of Asia. Thai Boxing, or muay Thai, is a prime example of an indigenous art that was handed down.

Vital ethnic traditions

Every ethnic group has developed one or more fighting styles or techniques. It's almost as though no ethnicity can exist as such unless it also manages to practice, transmit, and develop a fighting style with well-defined rules.

The table on the next page contains examples of names of ethnic combat styles, grouped under the generic term "wrestling," that are still in existence today, not just in their native regions but, in some cases, in a Western world always on the lookout for exotic practices:

Austria
Rangeln (Tirol)

Spain
Lucha canária
Lucha leon

Finland
Rintapaîni
Ritpaïni
Viopaîni

France
E vince (Corsica)
Gouren (Brittany)

Great Britain
Catch-as-catch-can
Cornwall
Cumberland
Devonshire
Lancashire
Loosehold
Norfolk
Shooting
Westmorland

Iceland
Glima

Portugal
Galfava

Switzerland
Schwingen

Sweden
Akseltag
Armtag
Belgtag
Beltescast
Biscast
Bondetag
Boukatag
Cragtag
Livtag
Rigcats

Albania
Mundje vençe

Armenia
Kokh

Azerbaijan
Gulesh

Bulgaria
Yagli gures

Daghestan
Khatkabi

Georgia
Ankoumara
Tchidaoba

Kazakhstan
Kures
Saïs

Kyrgyzstan
Koresh
Oodarch

Lithuania
Ristines

Moldova
Trinta dreapta
Trinta kunedika

Russia
"Belt wrestling"
"Né v skhvatkou"
Sombo

Serbia
Rvanje

Uzbekistan
Kurash

Tuva
Khuresh

Tajikistan
Gushti of Bukhara
Gutzanguiri

Turkmenistan
Gurech
Khiva

Turkey
Kusag gures
Yagli gures

Sakha
Kourdstan-tustuu
Khapsagai

Afghanistan
Kestik

Saudi Arabia
Istlish taban
Mossara taban
Moulapta

Burma
Letoussi
Nabast

China
Kio-li
Wushu

Korea
Ssirium-ha-ki

India
Azura
Bhimcencce
Djarazandj
Hanoumantée
Nara
Psarani pata

Indonesia
Pendjak-silette

Brazil
Capoeira (dance)

Iran
Guilan
Iliati
Kochti perse
Kordi
Mazendarani

Japan
Karasu-zumo
Konaki-zumo
Shinji-zumo
Toja-zumo

Malaysia
Berslate

Mongolia
Barilda
Bokh

Pakistan
Kushti

Philippines
Arias da mene

Thailand
Bando

Senegal
Béri
Olva
Laamb

Sudan
Toubata

Togo
Zvaha

As we can see, every ethnic group has developed its own combat techniques, which can be grouped under the term "wrestling." Now let's take a closer look at this discipline, which sports scholars and anthropologists, considered to be the ultimate primitive sport (in the sense of "primal"or ancestral).

Source: 100 Years of Olympic Wrestling (Raïko Petrov, FILA 1997)

Wrestling

Part Two: Wrestling— An Open Sport

This section provides an extensive overview of wrestling, which we call an "open sport" because the fighting styles described below flourish in an atmosphere of freedom of movement, location and time, without ring or enclosure, gloves or weapons, under many different forms, open to both sexes and all ages, and yet obeying very strict rules. This "openness" shouldn't be seen as a bad thing, but remember that no "wrestling" style is totally free of rules or restrictions. Naked and unarmed, the human body can become a veritable killing machine. Mortal combat is a myth, a figment of the collective imagination, even though such combats did once take place.

The history of wrestling

Wrestling is neither boxing nor a martial art. Historically speaking, it's at the origin of all types of "combat" where two bodies "measure" themselves against one another. It's an ancient, natural, "primal" sport that might even be called "rustic," requiring powers of observation and listening skills. It is an intellectual and, therefore, paradoxical sport.

Both as a sport and as a multi-millennial practice, wrestling has been part of every civilization and continues to exist today, whether at the Olympic or ethno-urban level, as an essential practice of pitting body against body. Unlike pro-wrestling or street fighting, this practice has its roots in a philosophy that is largely free of competitiveness, violence, and the excesses of modern culture normally associated with the "sports business."

"Fighters" Eadweard Muybridge, 1887

Wrestling is the antithesis of boxing. Bodies come together and catch hold of one another, but without heavy punches, blood, or excessive sweat. It's a "well-oiled" mechanism that follows rituals and rules accumulated over time. Wrestling is beautiful, from both an ethical and an aesthetic point of view, which is why it holds such fascination for the younger generation, regardless of gender or origin.

The first sport

Wrestling is a natural sport that's open to everyone, because it requires no special equipment or expensive facilities. Moreover, the division into weight classes gives every wrestler a chance to compete on an equal footing, whether male or female, and regardless of build or bodyweight. Wrestling also makes an important contribution to hygiene and physical training, as well as to education. It benefits the human organism in a variety of ways because training sessions and wrestling matches involve an entire range of physiological and psychological factors. It engages all the wrestler's muscle groups, joints, sense organs, intelligence, will, and overall personality.

With the possible exception of track and field, wrestling is the most ancient sport known to have been practiced competitively on a continual basis. Wrestling predates the ancient Olympic Games. Cave drawings of wrestlers from 3000 B.C. have been found in the remains of the Sumero-Akkadian civilization. Similar paintings exist from ancient Egyptian civilizations of around 2400 B.C. Wrestling became part of the Olympic Games in 708 B.C., shortly after the Games' recorded history began in 776 B.C. There were only three disciplines

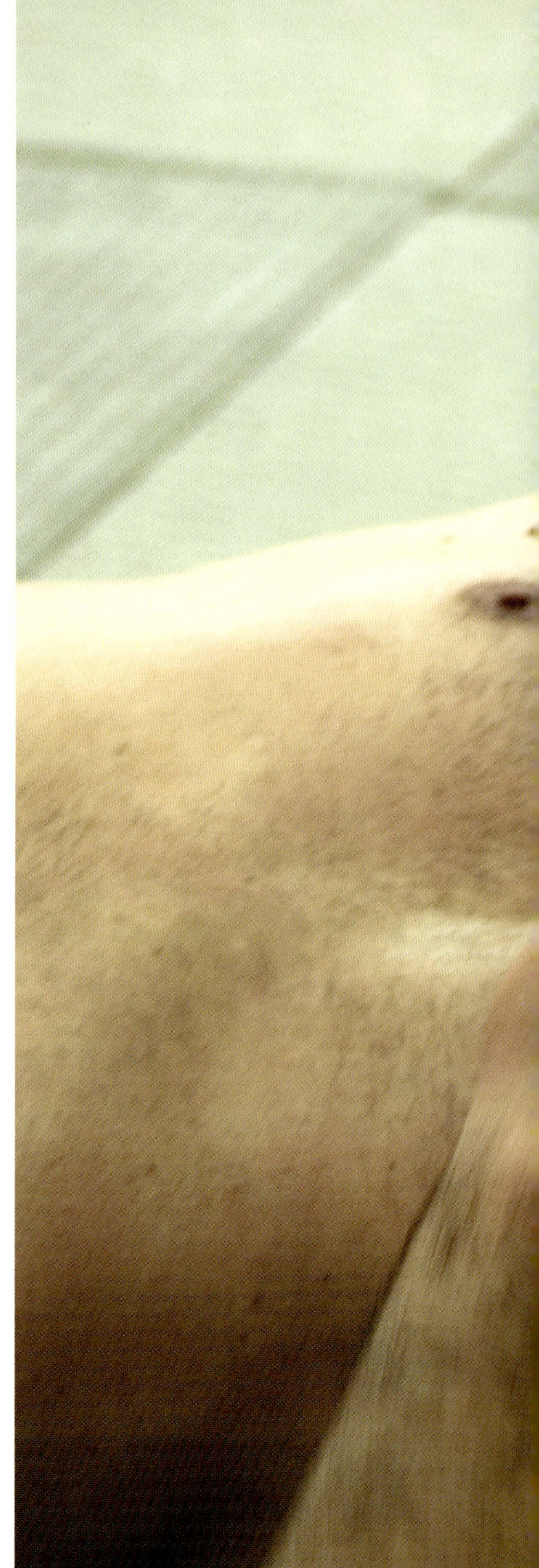

at that time, and generally two categories, not separated by weight but by age: *paides* (boys) and *andres* (men or adults). These age classes varied according to discipline, but also according to the Games, just as weight categories today vary from sport to sport. For "heavyweight" events (combat sports), contestants had to be over 14 years old. At 18 years, they became adult men.

The three martial ("heavyweight") disciplines represented at the Olympics (and other games) in ancient times were:

- "Orthia pale" wrestling, from 708 B.C. to 393 A.D.

- Pugilism, from 688 B.C. to 393 A.D. and

- Pankration, from 648 B.C. to 393 A.D.

The author Sextus Julius Africanus (third century A.D.) compiled a partial list of the champion athletes of his time, which has survived, thanks to Eusebius Pamphilus, bishop of Caesarea. Who can forget the wrestler Milo of Croton who won the Olympics in 540 B.C., only to be devoured by lions? A papyrus from Oxyrrhynchos furnished modern archeologists with fragmentary results of 263 Olympiads (of the 293 held between 776 B.C. and 393 A.D.) in 32 categories, for more than 170 cities, identifying a total of over 600 winners and 941 victories!

As an athletic discipline, modern sport wrestling exists in four styles:

- Greco-Roman wrestling

- Freestyle wrestling

- Women's wrestling

- Beach wrestling

Overall, modern wrestling is a system of bare-handed combat during which the adversaries use their bodies against each others'. The goal is either to "pin" both the opponent's shoulder blades to the mat or to win on points.

Let's take sombo, a combination of freestyle and judo. It was the most popular style in the republics of the former Soviet Union, but has not yet been accepted as an Olympic sport. Freestyle wrestling is similar to the "folkstyle" wrestling practiced in many American schools. The holds are relatively limited, are not dangerous, and can be applied to any part of the body. Greco-Roman wrestling limits holds to the upper body.

Wrestling was on the program of the first modern Olympic Games in Athens in 1896. It was even the symbol of the games and return to the Greek and Roman ideal. Freestyle and Greco-Roman wrestling have been practiced regularly at the Olympics since 1920. Today, Russia dominates wrestling in the Greco-Roman category. The United States is close behind in freestyle. Other countries also produce international wrestlers of a high caliber, including Iran, Turkey, and Mongolia, where wrestling is also their national sport. In 1904, the Olympic organizers added a second type of wrestling, not as charged with history or splendor, but hugely popular. Generally known as "catch-as-catch-can," this freestyle wrestling became a staple at nineteenth century fairs and festivals in Great Britain and the United States. It's a form of professional entertainment, a description of which can be found in *Gangs of New York* by Herbert Asbury (1856, adapted for the screen). Like Greco-Roman wrestling, it has become a staple of the Games themselves. The year

Championship poster, Paris 1899

1912 saw the creation of the International Federation of Associated Wrestling Styles (FILA), which is currently based in Lausanne, Switzerland and merges 154 affiliated federations that organize junior and senior world and continental championships in Greco-Roman, freestyle and women's wrestling. The first freestyle wrestling world championship took place in Helsinki in 1951. By 2004, there were over 80 million wrestlers in the world, with more than 210 nations participating in wrestling at the Olympic and traditional level.

Wrestling style: moves and techniques

In the two main wrestling styles (Greco-Roman and freestyle), the wrestlers start the match on their feet and try to takedown their opponent, using holds to pin the person to the mat.

Greco-Roman wrestling strictly forbids grasping the opponent below the belt, tripping him, or actively using one's legs to perform any action. In ancient Greece, brutal wrestling matches were the high point of the Olympic Games. The Romans borrowed freely from Greek wrestling, but eliminated the brutality, producing what is now known as Greco-Roman wrestling.

In freestyle wrestling, on the other hand, the wrestler can grab the opponent's legs or use his own to attack.

Both wrestling styles prohibit twisting, stretching, or exerting any dangerous holds. Wrestling is a "manly" sport requiring total—but not brutal—physical contact. It's also a game.

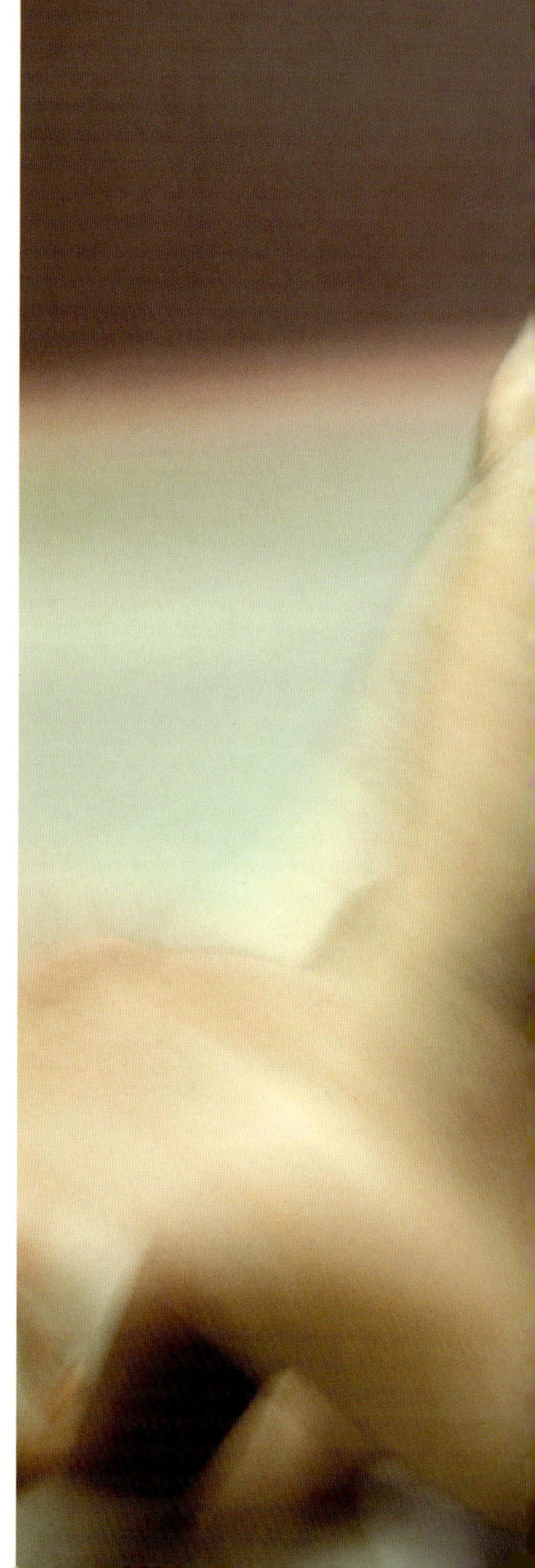

The wrestlers step onto the mat. The referee checks that their fingernails are short so they won't scratch each other, and makes sure they each have a handkerchief.

The mat

Wrestling matches take place on a 10- x 10-meter mat. A red circle (or any other highly visible color) designates the competition area. A FILA-approved mat has a 9-meter diameter, surrounded by a 1.5-meter border of the same thickness. A one-meter-wide red band that also forms an integral part of the wrestling area is drawn around the circumference of the 9-meter circle. A central circle forms the mat center (one-meter diameter). The area of the mat lying inside the red band is the central wrestling surface (7-meter diameter). The red band is the "passivity zone." To prevent contamination, the mat must be washed and disinfected before every wrestling session (very important in schools, because scholastic wrestling is highly regulated in the West). A circle must be traced in the middle of the mat with an inside diameter of one meter and a surrounding band 10-centimeters wide. The color of this 10-centimeter band and that of the band marking off the wrestling area must be red.

In ancient times, the wrestler's body was naked and slightly oiled.

Today, equipment for a competition (as for any type of match) consists of:

▪ One reversible red/blue wrestling singlet or two singlets, one red and one blue, generally made of lycra, which can also comprise elastic trunks or shorts (regional wrestling, beach wrestling).

The division into weight classes gives every wrestler a chance to compete on an equal footing, whether male or female, and regardless of build or body weight.

- One pair of socks (except for beach wrestling or wrestling on sand, in which case the feet must be bare).
- One pair of wrestling shoes extending above the ankles. The laces must be firmly fixed to the shoes with tape or similar material.
- Light kneepads may be worn that do not contain any metal.
- Wrestlers must present themselves before the match and carry on a cloth handkerchief throughout the match.
- Ear protection is permitted, but no genital protection.
- Long hair is not recommended.

Weight categories

Wrestlers compete on the basis of their weight category. Classified by age, the weight categories for all situations (amateur, semi-pro, high-level competition) are as follows:

#	Schoolboys	Cadets	Juniors	Seniors
1	29–32 kg	39–42 kg	46–50 kg	50–55 kg
2	35 kg	46 kg	55 kg	60 kg
3	38 kg	50 kg	60 kg	66 kg
4	42 kg	54 kg	66 kg	74 kg
5	47 kg	58 kg	74 kg	84 kg
6	53 kg	63 kg	84 kg	96 kg
7	59 kg	69 kg	96 kg	96–120 kg
8	66 kg	76 kg	96–120 kg	
9	73 kg	85 kg		
10	73–85 kg	85–100 kg		

Sources: Fila

At the Olympic level—for example, at the 2000 Games in Sydney—the wrestling program changed. As of 1972, wrestling was divided into 10 classes each, in freestyle and Greco-Roman. During the Sydney Games, however, only eight classes competed in each style. The weights were also altered slightly, and the lightest class, usually called "light flyweight," was eliminated.

WEIGHT CATEGORIES (2000)

Men's Categories	Women's Categories
55 kg	48 kg
60 kg	51 kg
66 kg	55 kg
74 kg	59 kg
84 kg	63 kg
96 kg	67 kg
120 kg	72 kg
97 – 130 kg	

Sources: Fila

A typical wrestling match (in this case, Greco-Roman)

First of all, the wrestlers must greet one another (by shaking hands).

The match consists of three periods of two minutes each. The wrestler winning two of these periods is declared the victor. A period comprises one minute of wrestling in a standing position and 2 x 30 seconds of wrestling in a compulsory "par terre" position. The match starts in the center of the mat

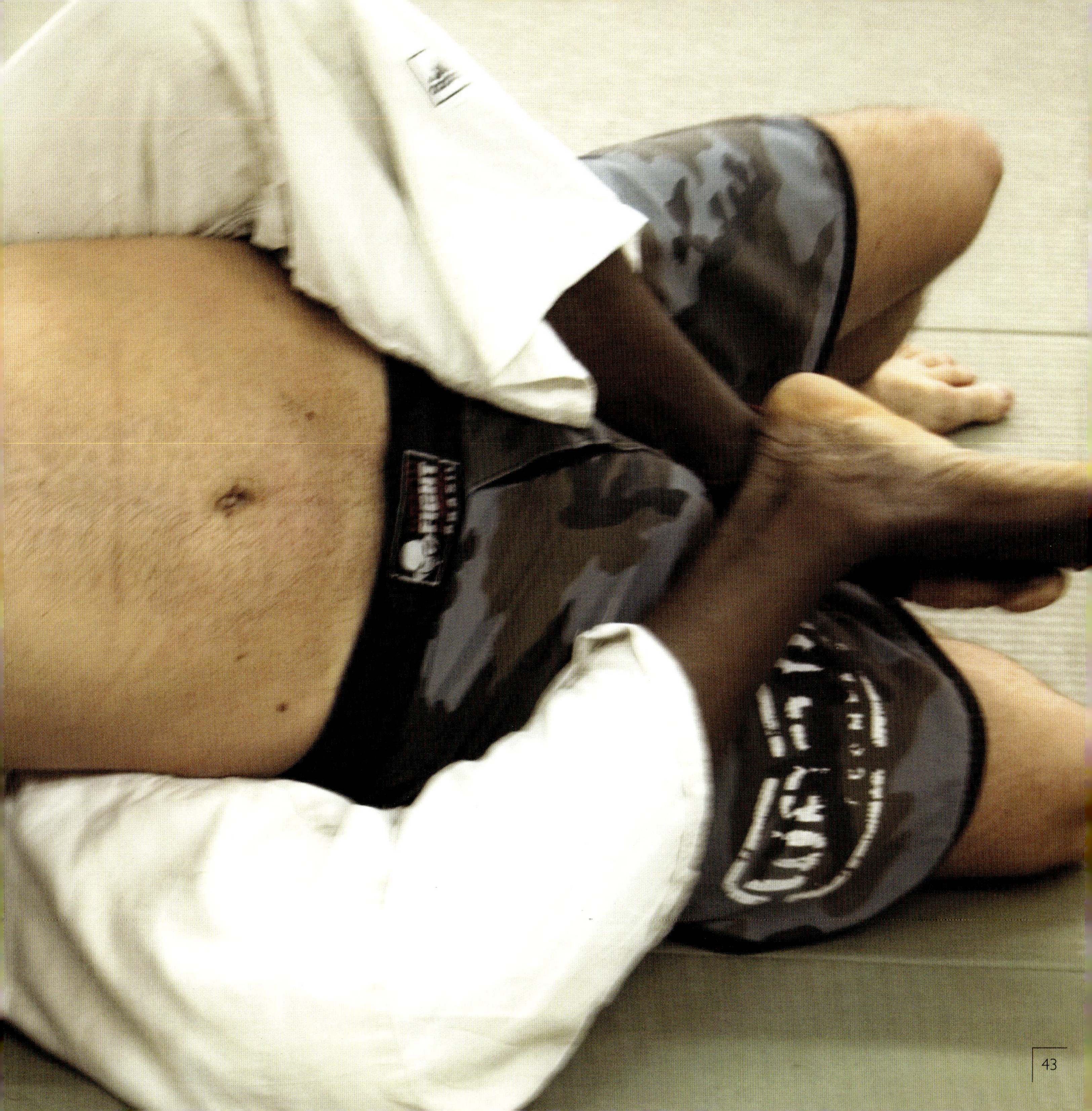

in a standing position. The wrestlers can perform any authorized actions. After one minute of fighting, the referee stops the match and designates one wrestler who will perform the ordered hold in the par terre position. The first wrestler to execute the ordered hold wins the match at this moment (according to the criteria established for winning a match). If neither of the two wrestlers scores a technical point, the referee will draw lots. The wrestler who wins the drawing will be the first to execute the ordered hold.

Holds

Following the shaking of hands, the referee signals the two wrestlers to start wrestling. Below is an overview of a number of basic holds with various definitions of moves (or blocking positions) and the different actions possible in a standard match. There are two positions: standing and par terre. The intermediate position ("on all fours"), which brings the wrestler to the ground, is considered part of the "standing" position.

Standing

Body lock: A hold in which a wrestler locks arms around the torso of his opponent and tries to throw him to the mat.

Single-leg takedown: A move in which a wrestler takes down his opponent by lifting his opponent's leg with his arm.

Double-leg takedown: A move in which a wrestler takes down his opponent by attacking both his legs.

Takedown: The act of bringing an opponent from a standing position down to the mat.

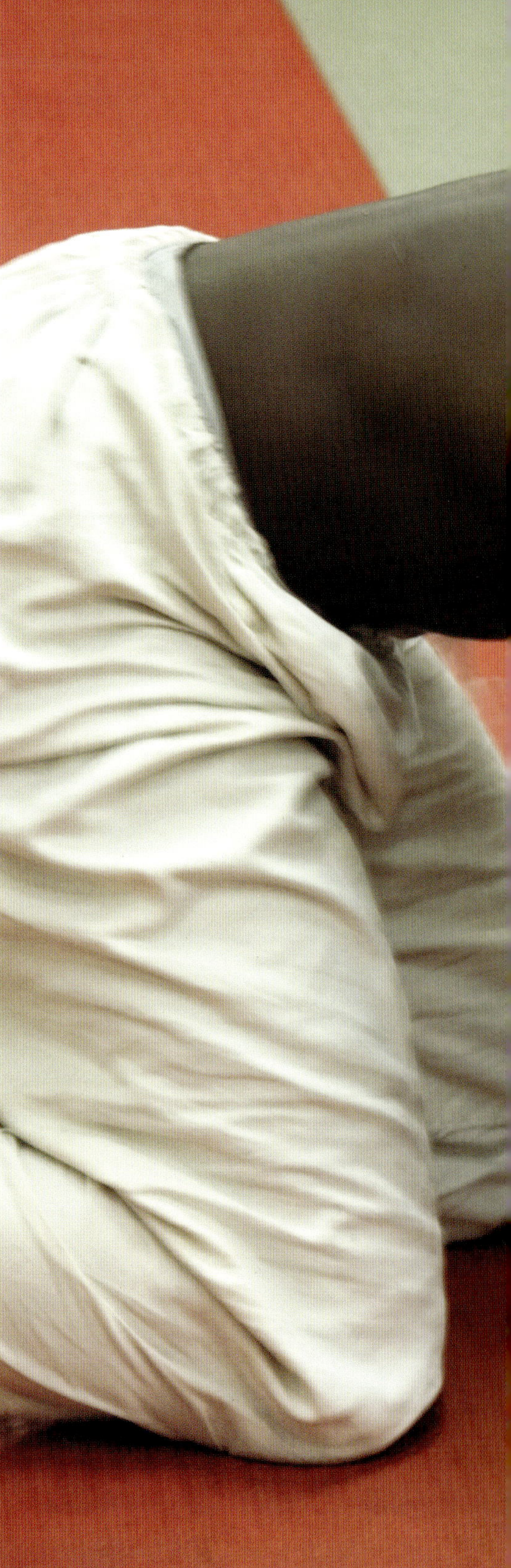

Bridge: The arched position a wrestler adopts with his back facing the mat to avoid having his shoulders touch the mat.

Arm control: Controlling the opponent's arms.

Par terre

Body throw: A move in which a wrestler locks his arms around the body of his opponent and throws him to the mat.

Belly-to-back suplex: A hold in which a wrestler throws his opponent in a wide arc of movement while holding him from behind.

Gut wrench: A move in which a wrestler goes into the bridge position and rolls his opponent over his own torso onto his back.

Ankle lace: A hold in which a wrestler blocks his opponent's ankles with his arms and exposes his back to the mat.

Grapevine: A move in which a wrestler uses his legs to turn his opponent (mainly par terre but, in freestyle wrestling, can also be executed while standing).

Danger position: A position in which a wrestler's back is at less than a 90 degree angle to the mat.

Referee's position: On the mat, the starting position in which one wrestler has his hands and knees on the mat, and the other wrestler is kneeling beside him with two hands on his back.

Grand amplitude: A throw in which an opponent's center of gravity is higher than that of a wrestler who is trying to throw him.

Arm throw: A move in which a wrestler throws his opponent over his shoulder by holding the opponent's arm.

Bridge out: An escape move in which a wrestler rolls from a bridge onto his stomach.

Fall: The act of pinning an opponent's shoulders to the mat.

Actions

Wrestling consists of two actions, the hold and the fall.

Fall (or pin)

A wrestler scores a "fall" (pin) when he pins both his opponent's shoulders against the mat long enough for the referee to observe total control. When the fall takes place at the edge of the mat, both shoulders must be in full contact with the passivity zone; the head may not be touching the protection area. A fall in the protection area is not valid. If the wrestler is pinned on both shoulders as a consequence of his own violation of the rules or of an illegal hold for which he is responsible, the fall will be considered valid for his opponent. The fall is valid when the judge or mat chairman agrees with the referee's opinion. If the referee does not signal the fall and the fall is valid, it may be declared with the consent of the judge and mat chairman. To be observed and recognized, the fall must be clearly maintained, meaning that the wrestler's two shoulders must be simultaneously touching the mat during the short period of stoppage specified in the first paragraph, even in the case of a belly-to-back suplex. In all cases, the referee will strike the mat only after he has obtained confirmation from the judge or, failing this, from the mat chairman. The referee will then blow his whistle to end the match.

Danger position

A wrestler is in the danger position when the line of his shoulders or back forms an angle with the mat that is less than 90 degrees, and when he resists with his upper body to avoid a fall (see definition of "fall").

Grand amplitude hold

Any action or hold performed by a wrestler in the standing position is considered to be a grand amplitude hold when it causes the opponent to lose all contact with the ground, controls him, makes him describe a broad, sweeping curve in the air, and brings him to the ground in a direct and immediate danger position. In the par terre position, any complete lift from the ground executed by the attacking wrestler is also considered a grand amplitude hold, whether the attacked wrestler lands belly down or in a danger position.

The danger position is worth more points than the grand amplitude hold. Consequently, a fall scores the greatest number of points and can be considered the goal of wrestling.

Winning

A match can be won as follows:

a) By a "fall"

b) Injury, withdrawal, default, or disqualification of the opponent. At the end of each period, one wrestler must be declared the winner. The wrestler winning two periods is declared the winner of the match. If a victory can be declared after two periods, the third period is canceled.

c) On technical superiority

d) On points (based on an approved or agreed-upon scale)

Officials

For all types of wrestling, the following officials must be present:

- One referee who prevents wrestlers from leaving the mat and executing illegal holds.
- One mat chairman (or referee's assistant) who validates and counts points.
- Every competition must also have an approved judge to mark points.

The referee monitors the time, can encourage wrestlers to wrestle more actively (*dawai*) or adopt more open wrestling tactics (*open*), can warn a wrestler who refuses to assume the ordered position (*attention*), request a penalty, etc. In the case of a tie, the referee draws lots.

Prohibitions

Wrestlers are not allowed to:

- Pull hair, ears, genitals or nipples, pinch, bite, twist fingers, toes, or generally to perform any actions, gestures, or holds with the intention of torturing the opponent or making him suffer in order to force him to withdraw.
- Kick, head-butt, choke, push, and use holds that may endanger the opponent's life, or may fracture or dislocate limbs, step on the opponent's feet or touch his face between the eyebrows and line of the mouth.
- Thrust an elbow or knee into the opponent's stomach or abdomen, carry out any twisting action that is likely to cause suffering, or hold the opponent by his singlet.
- Cling to or grasp the mat.
- Speak during the match.
- Grab the sole of the opponent's foot (grabbing the upper part of the foot or heel is allowed).
- Agree on an outcome to the match between themselves.

Refusing to fight (fleeing a hold) and evading gives points to the opponent.

With the possible exception of track and field, wrestling is the most ancient sport known to have been practiced competitively on a continual basis.

Deadly holds

All matches must have an observer or referee who prohibits the following behaviors that could endanger a wrestler's life or health:

- Holding the throat

- Twisting an arm by more than 90 degrees

- Applying a forearm lock

- Holding the opponent's head or neck with both hands, and any situation or position causing strangulation

- Executing a double nelson (unless executed from the side, without using the legs on any part of the opponent's body)

- Bringing the opponent's arm behind his back while applying pressure to it in a position where the forearm forms an acute angle

- Executing a hold by stretching the opponent's spinal column

- Executing a cravate with one or both hands in any direction whatsoever (the only holds allowed involve the head and one arm)

- Lifting an opponent in a bridge position and throwing him to the mat (severe impact on the ground); in other words, a bridge must be forced down; and

- Breaking a bridge by pushing in the direction of the opponent's head

Women's wrestling

Women's wrestling has been growing on the competitive level since the beginning of the twentieth century. Matches between women have existed since the dawn of time (see below). They have been the object of fantasies and entertainment for men (and women!), and have had commercial offshoots. Rules for women's wrestling are very strict, with the following characteristics:

Age

The age categories are:

Schoolgirls: 14/15 years (as of age 13 with a medical certificate and parental permission)

Cadets: 16/17 years (as of age 15 with a medical certificate and parental permission)

Juniors: 18/20 years (as of age 17 with a medical certificate and parental permission)

Seniors: 20 years and older

Weight

#	Schoolgirls	Cadets	Juniors	Seniors
1	28–30 kg	36–38 kg	40–44 kg	44–48 kg
2	32 kg	40 kg	48 kg	51 kg
3	34 kg	43 kg	51 kg	55 kg
4	37 kg	46 kg	55 kg	59 kg
5	40 kg	49 kg	59 kg	63 kg
6	44 kg	52 kg	63 kg	67 kg
7	48 kg	56 kg	67 kg	67–72 kg
8	52 kg	60 kg	67–72 kg	
9	57 kg	65 kg		
10	57–62 kg	65–70 kg		

Sources: Fila

By 2004, there were
over 80 million
wrestlers in the world,
with more than 210
nations participating
in wrestling at
the Olympic and
traditional level.

Note: Women weighing more than 72 kilograms are not eliminated or prohibited from wrestling. They can be classified as "at large" or can integrate wrestling practices appropriate to their weight.

Dress

The same rules apply as for the men except:

■ An underwire bra may not be worn and

■ It is forbidden to wear earrings, barrettes, bracelets, rings or any rigid or metal object, or to wear a man's singlet or low-cut shirt.

Illegal holds

Same as for the men, plus all double nelsons in the "par terre" or standing position.

The grand champions

The Swedish wrestler Johan Richthoff was the first freestyle heavyweight to retain his title (in 1928 and 1932). The Estonian wrestler Kristian Palusalu competed in both Greco-Roman and freestyle wrestling in the 1936 Olympics. The Soviet wrestler Aleksandr Medved won three consecutive Olympic titles: in 1964 in the "light heavyweight" category, in 1968 in the "heavyweight" category, and in 1972 in the "super heavyweight" category. The Hungarian Istvan Kozma was the first to win two gold medals, in 1964 and 1968, in Greco-Roman wrestling. As successor to his fellow countryman Medved, the Soviet wrestler Soslan Andiyev won two golds in freestyle wrestling, in 1976 and 1980. During these same years another Soviet, Aleksandr Kolchinsky, won two golds in Greco-Roman wrestling. U.S. wrestler Bruce Baumgartner, in a career that spanned four Olympiads, won two golds in freestyle wrestling, in 1984 and 1992. Aleksandr Karelin was the first to win three golds in Greco-Roman wrestling (1988, 1992, and 1996), equaling his fellow countryman and counterpart in freestyle wrestling, Medved.

Although France has not won the gold since Berlin in 1936 (Emile Poilve, freestyle), Ghani Yolouz, now an Olympic trainer, won the silver for Greco-Roman wrestling in Atlanta in 1996 along with Daniel Robin, who won the silver in Mexico in 1968 (Greco-Roman and freestyle). Finally, when women's freestyle wrestling debuted at the 2004 Olympic Games in Athens, the French wrestlers Anna Gomis and Lise Legrand (55 and 63 kilograms) won the bronze. Two women wrestlers from Japan, Yoshida Saori and Icho Kaori, the Ukrainian Irini Merleni, and the Chinese wrestler Wang Xu, all won the gold.

Local wrestling styles

As we said before, every ethnic group tends to develop its own wrestling style with its own unique characteristics both in terms of tradition (dress, rituals, accessories) and holds. Such styles are often the expression of a strong regional or national identity (such as Corsican or Breton). They may involve other arts (for example, dance). It would be beyond the scope of this book to examine all these characteristics. There is an international association of regional wrestling (region in the sense of ethnic and historic) that organizes annual competitions where amateur wrestlers come together and compete.

Every ethnic group in the world has developed one or more unique forms of single combat.

None of these wrestling styles is recognized by the Olympic Committee. Nevertheless, freestyle wrestling was originally inspired by everything that was not Greco-Roman, including any style that permitted the use of the lower limbs or judo-like moves. Generally speaking, all wrestling styles are derived from either Greco-Roman or freestyle.

Below we offer several ethnographic "anecdotes" related to these wrestling styles, also known as regional, traditional, or native (as the Anglo-Saxons call them) styles:

Sub-Saharan Africa

In northern Benin, a form of wrestling continues to be practiced by adolescents returning from the fields who want to test their bravery. A similar style is found in neighboring Senegal (*béri*). In Niger, wrestling is the most popular sport, beating out soccer.

Celtic wrestling

Called "gouren" in Brittany, this form of wrestling is performed on sand with bare feet, bare torsos, and black kneepants ("pantacourt"). This same wrestling style is also found in Britain, Ireland, and even northern Spain. All these variations are governed by one European association, which holds an annual championship meet. In 2005, Niger hosted the first international contest of traditional wrestling.

Sombo

Throughout the twentieth century, sombo was considered the number-one combat sport in the Soviet Union. It was introduced by the Soviet government in the early 1920s for the purpose of developing a nationalistic art of self-defense worthy of its name. In fact, Sombo was an attempt to unite all the regional wrestling styles, which were studied and identified by the People's Commissioners, and to combine their different aspects in a uniform whole in order to prepare and politicize the nation's youth. The name is an acronym of SOM-oborona Bes Orusyia (self-defense without weapons). A careful examination of the rules shows that sombo is a synthesis of various methods derived from jujitsu, American and French freestyle, and English and French boxing. Today, more than 50 years after the death of Stalin, the art of Sombo is being taught around the world, and Russia largely dominates all wrestling competitions.

Turkey

What the world finds most fascinating about "Gures" (Turkish for "close, bare-handed combat with the bare hands") is the practice of covering the body with oil ("yagli"), which was very widespread in Greco-Roman antiquity because it made holds difficult to execute, protected the body, etc. According to the Persian legend of Kirkpinar, this sport originated in the fifteenth century when Sultan Orhan lost two of his most courageous warriors. During an encampment, these soldiers were unable to stop wrestling and were found dead of exhaustion the following morning. Each year, various competitions are orga-

Senegalese Wrestling, Yekini

Turkish Oil Wrestling

nized in Turkey and adjacent countries exclusively for men aged 14 and older. The ceremonies generally begin with the "peshrev" (a warm-up dance), the "pehlivan" (hero), and the "kispet" (the short pants worn). The master of ceremonies or referee is called the "cazgir." In recent years, France has hosted oil wrestling events and there are even clubs devoted to it, particularly in the Turkish community.

Mongolia

During the month of July, the festival of Nadaam (meaning "game" or "competition") is held in Oulan-Bator and elsewhere. There are three competitions: archery, horse racing, and wrestling. Like Sumo wrestling in Japan, Mongolian wrestling is considered to be an artform. Before each match, the wrestlers present themselves to the crowd by performing an eagle dance in their traditional costume (thick boots, embroidered shorts, a sort of bolero with straps covering their arms and back, and a silk cap) and then uncover their heads. The ground can be covered with grass, gravel, or sand. The rules are simple: the first one to takedown his opponent is declared the winner and moves on to the next round. Men of all shapes and sizes compete against one another in this event. There are nine rounds. The wrestler who wins five rounds in a row is awarded the title of falcon. He who wins six rounds becomes an elephant. The winner of the overall competition is a lion. The lion who wins two years in a row becomes a titan. A titan who wins a third time is called a national titan. If he is strong enough to win a fourth year in a row, he is declared invincible!

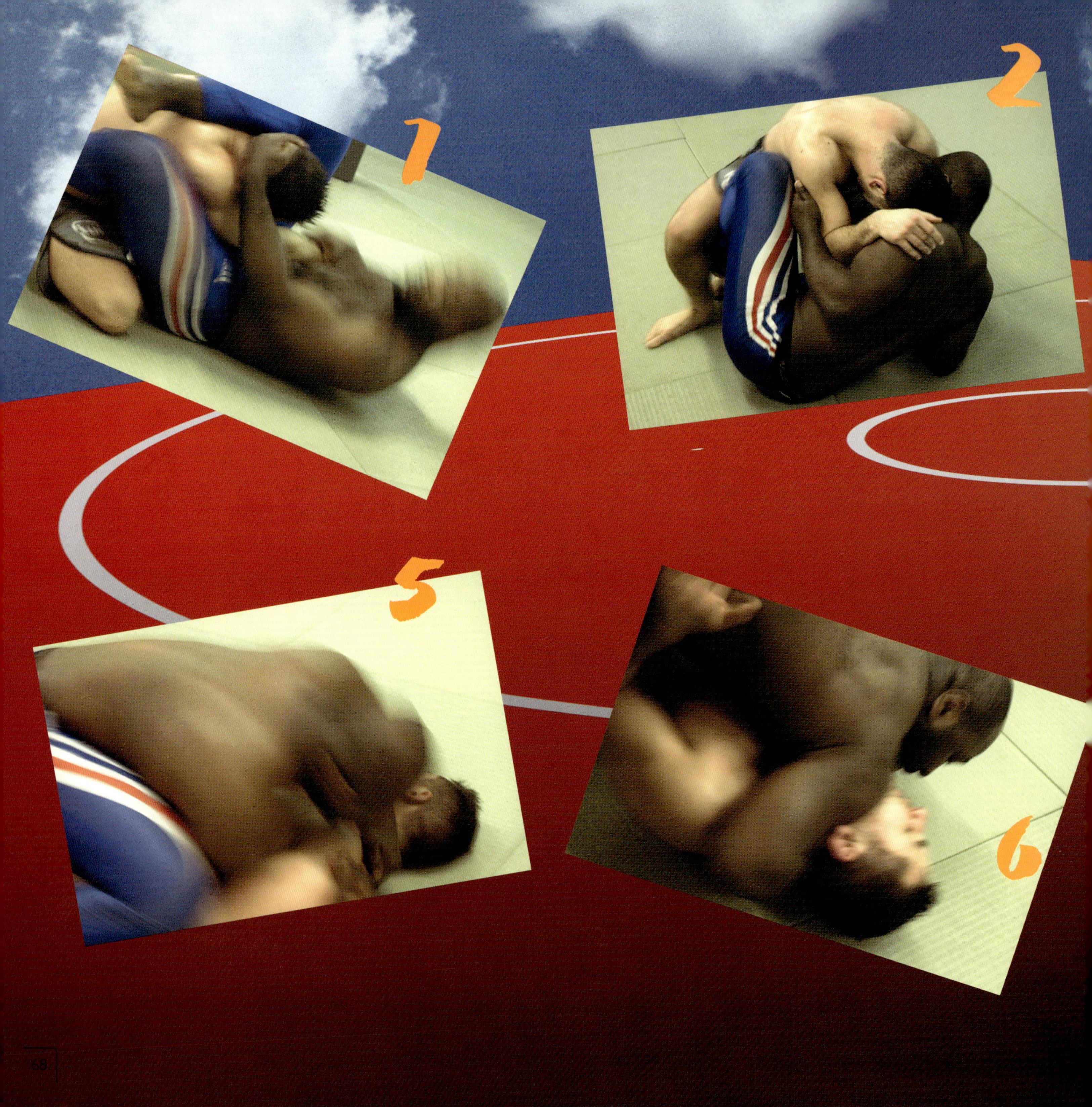
1
2
5
6

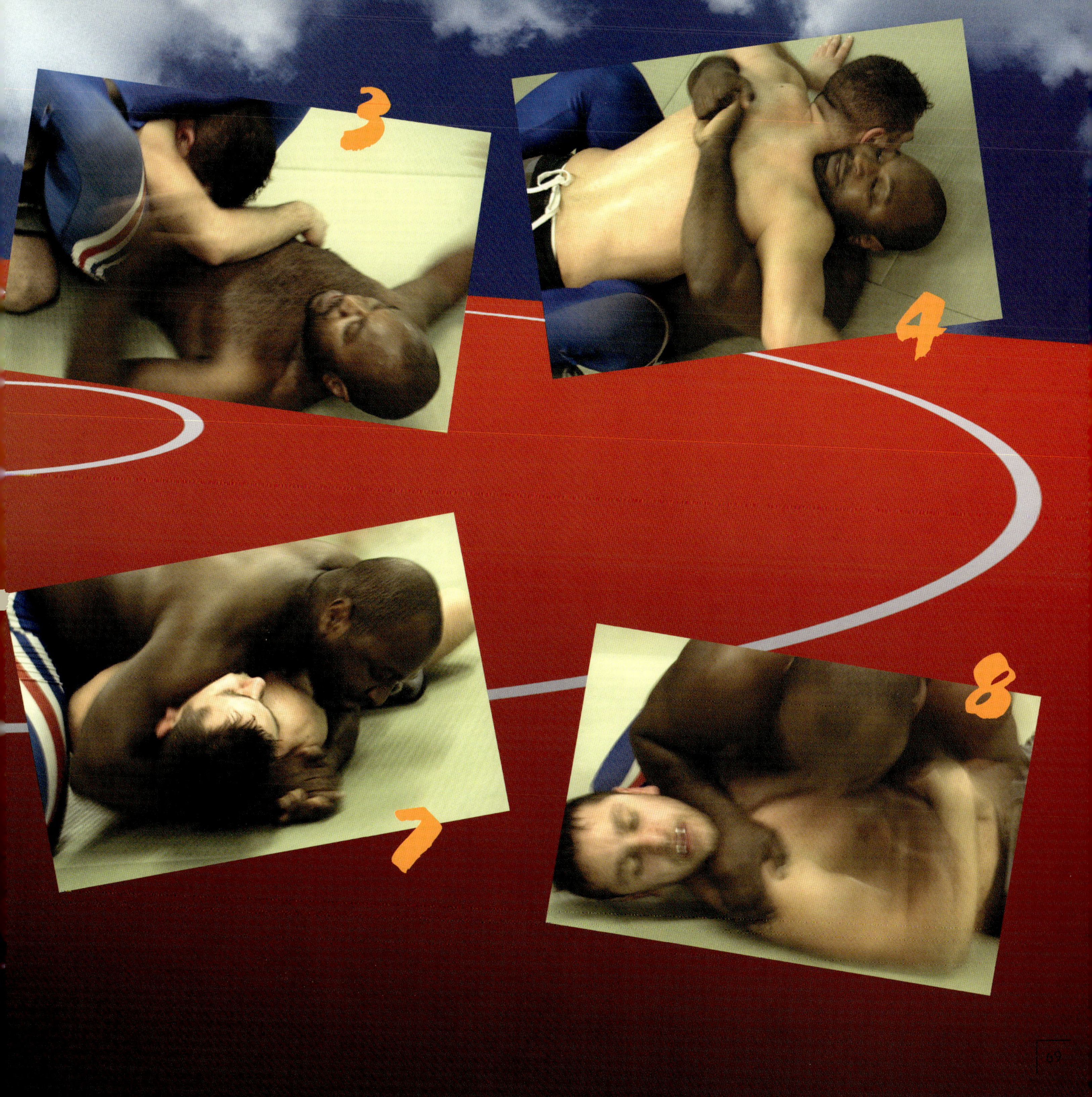
3
4
7
8

India

Kushti, once considered a royal sport, is the most popular and ancient form of traditional wrestling in all of India, where the oldest styles of combat and martial arts have been recorded and continue to exist today. Kushti is also practiced in Pakistan and requires a tremendous amount of physical training. Future wrestlers are recruited at a very young age and must dedicate themselves to Kushti, day and night. They practically form a caste. Supervised by a guru, these men meet in "akharas" (gymnasiums or, literally, "square arenas," referring to the shape of the combat area) where they learn endurance (diet, the ability to withstand pain, and deprivation), undergo trials (carrying a millstone), and practice the different moves (sometimes similar to yoga). Wrestlers are practically nude, with only a cotton cloth covering their loins. They must stay celibate for as long as they remain in the akhara. Leaving is the equivalent of permanent exile and can result in death by self-denial (starvation or sleep deprivation) and ostracism.

Japan

More popular than soccer in France, sumo wrestling has been practiced in Japan for over 2000 years by men of above-average strength and agility. It began as an ancient agricultural ritual of prayers for a good harvest. Although it originally involved total, mortal combat without rules, it became much more subdued in the late nineteenth century. The average sumo wrestler (also called "sumotori") is 1.85 meters tall and weighs 150 kilograms. Some are as large as 250 kilograms and over 2-meters tall. Coaches are trained to scout the young

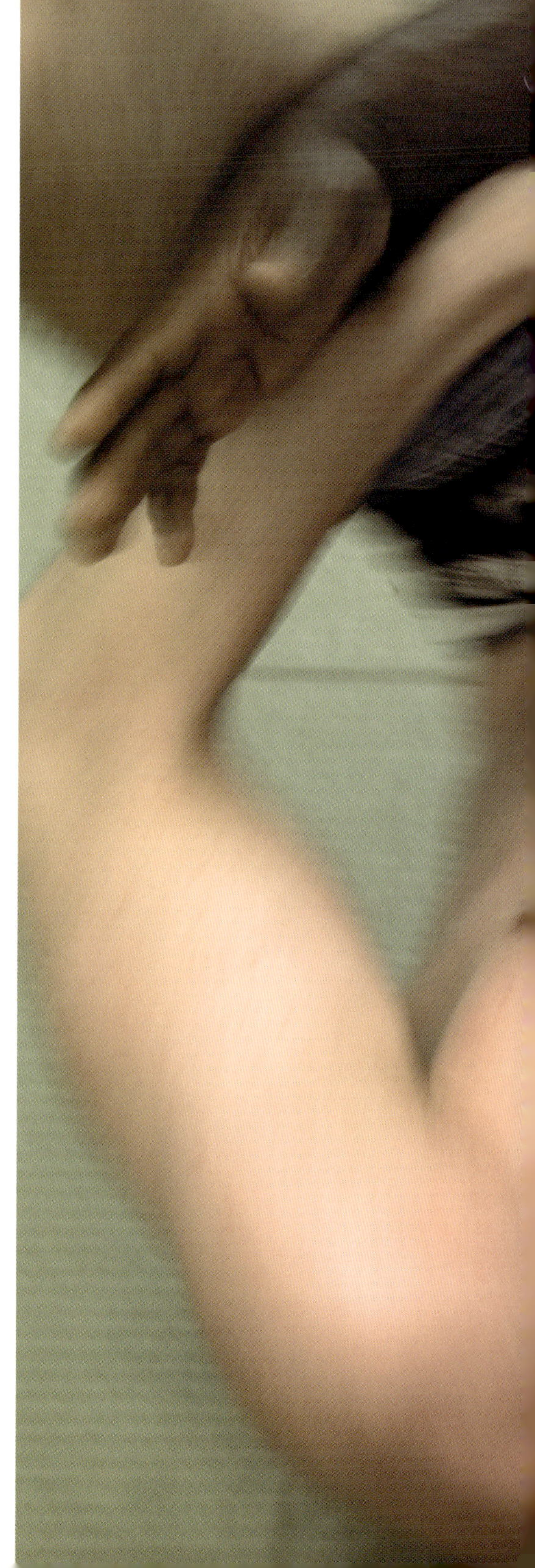

for future champions; sumotori are said to be born and not made. Matches take place in a ring (*dohyo*). The two wrestlers begin by squatting face-to-face with fists resting on the ground, staring directly into one another's eyes. Then, suddenly, they slap both fists on the ground and charge. If the collision itself isn't enough to throw one of the sumotori off balance, they need to come up with an immediate strategy, either for causing the other to fall, or for pushing him outside the circle, in order to claim the victory. There are nearly 100 techniques for throwing and unbalancing an opponent. Sumo wrestling is extremely hierarchical, with 11 divisions culminating in the yokozuna (highest stage, equivalent to "demi-god"). The yokozuna is the object of adoration and pampering for the rest of his life. Training conditions are similar to those of kushti wrestlers, except that sumotori must follow a diet designed to put on weight. There are many fans of this sport from around the world!

Mexico

Called *lucha libre* or Mexican wrestling, this sport has nothing to do with the American WWE, which appears to be nothing but a form of entertainment (paid and profitable, thanks to betting) at the expense of the sport. In Mexico, the wrestlers (*luchadores*) are masked, mysterious, unknown, and pseudony-mous (Blue Demon, Perro Aguayo), but extremely popular. They generally come from the country's poorest regions, are close to the people, and often serve as an inspiration to children (which is where the myth of Zorro came from). Mexican wrestlers are true heroes, dressed in flashy tights and capes, and competing in masks (a symbol borrowed by Subcomandante Marcos).

The Mexican Magazine "Lucha Libre"
(Free-style fighting) 1950

The rules are simple: everything is legal except striking below the belt. The point is to pin the opponent to the mat for three seconds (counted down by one or two judges), or "punish" him (with locks or holds) until he surrenders. The match is divided into three rounds (or *caídas*), and one of the wrestlers must win two out of three. These rounds have no time limits. Today, Mexican wrestling is administered by two organizations: the *Consejo Mundial de Lucha Libre* (CMLL) and the Triple A (AAA). The latter is exclusively Mexican, whereas the former includes wrestlers from Puerto Rico, Brazil, and even Japan, countries where many Mexican wrestlers have gone to train and make a name for themselves. The wrestler's main objective is to unmask his rival or force him to shave his head (acts of humiliation). A wrestler can be either a *técnico* ("technician" or good guy) or a rudo ("tough" or bad guy). The wrestlers' trophies are basically masks and hair (*máscara y cabellera*). Each wrestler has an archrival (the wrestler's number-one foe), the most famous archenemies being El Santo and the Blue Demon. These two wrestlers were made famous by their appearances in films. Even though they're both gone, they're still frightening as myths and icons, with masks resembling skulls, a recurring symbol in Mexican folklore.

Brazil

Capoeira or "fighting dance," which is one of the most popular wrestling styles in the world today, is both game and dance. There are two main types: "capoeira Angola" and "capoeira regional." According to the Frenchman Arno Mansouri, "A large part of [capoeira's] culture is still transmitted orally." The capoeirista is a combination athlete, dancer, acrobat, practical joker, comedian, and musician. From a historical point of view, it resulted from the extraordinary coming together (forced proximity) of different African cultures on Brazilian soil during 300 years of slavery. The slaves imported their dances, rituals, festivals, and songs from Africa and ended up creating a unique ritual based on their situation in Brazil. Although the dancing and singing appeared harmless to masters and overseers, they were actually preparation for combat between the weakest, least powerful, and the strongest.

For a long time capoeira was outlawed and suppressed, even after slavery was abolished, but it was finally legalized by the Brazilian government in 1937. It's still being taught and practiced, not only in schools and on the streets, but also at universities, theater and modern dance workshops, circus schools, and sports centers in Brazil, the United States and, more recently, in Europe. It is above all a ritual of great beauty.

In their movements, the capoeiristas are imitating animals. Macaque monkeys, reptiles, and cats perform maneuvers while right-side up, upside-down, on all fours or lying flat, ready to leap into the air or onto their prey. They're supported on all sides by the other capoeiristas who, while waiting their turn, form a circle around them and "warm up" the game with rhythmic percussion, songs, and clapping. This circle is the "roda" and inside it is the play area, the place for dancing and wrestling. This is the arena in which they show off, expose themselves to danger, try on different personalities, and establish a physical dialog with their partner (or adversary). Like all games, capoeira has its traditions, rules, and codes for entering the circle, stopping or starting up again. As soon as capoeiristas reach the center and face their opponent, however, they must watch their step. Anything can happen in an instant, even when the rhythm is slow. While at the center, they're alone in a unique experience that will never be repeated. If a capoeirista is distracted by a thought, it can inhibit his or her reflexes. The idea is to keep from touching the opponent, remain fluid, and stop a movement before encountering an obstacle. In the end, there are neither winners nor losers. The opponents shake hands and stop there. Similarities have been noted between capoeirista rituals and ethno-urban, hip-hop acrobatics.

Fighting games between Brazilian Indians, Photograph 1900

Capoiera

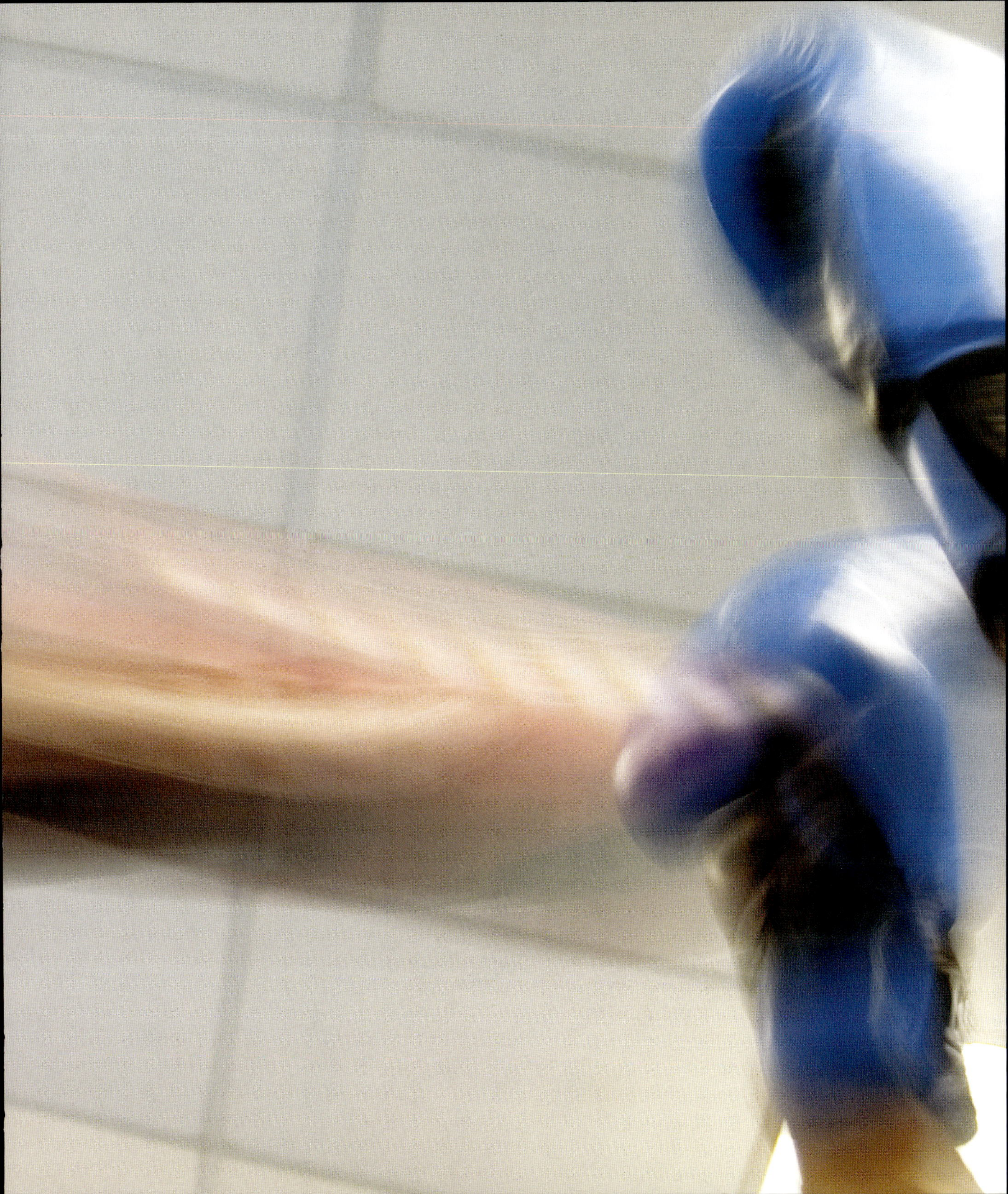

Boxing

Leaving behind the original, primal "circle" that gave birth to all forms of sport wrestling and all the rituals of close combat, let's move on to the "ring," which is actually an enclosed square. Within this space, the opponents must maintain their distance, remain standing, and strike one another, sometimes until there's a knockout (KO). The greatest difference between this and the wrestling styles we examined above is that every part of the upright body is offered as a target.

The birth of boxing

Boxing is a combat sport in which two adversaries face each other and punch. A boxing match follows established rules and procedures and is supervised by a referee, judges, and a timekeeper. The participants' primary goal is to punch their opponent's face and torso until they fall to the ground and remain there for more than 10 seconds; in other words, a knockout or KO. Consequently, the science of combat in this case consists in avoiding being hit. "It is the art of throwing more punches than you receive," (A. Philonenko). Many matches, however, are played for points. Blows below the belt are illegal. The main offensive punches are the *hook*, *jab*, *cross*, and *uppercut*. The *guard* position is when the arms and legs are ready both to defend and attack.

Ancient boxing or pugilism had fewer rules than there are today. There were no rounds. The boxers simply hit one another until one of them was either knocked out or admitted defeat. Unlike current boxing rules, there was no rule against hitting an opponent who was down. Instead of wearing gloves,

The first World Boxing Championship,
John L. Sullivan, 1880

boxers in antiquity wrapped leather straps (called *himantes* or *myrmex*) around their hands and fists, leaving their fingers unprotected (this is under dispute). Pugilism was the precursor of English boxing, which appeared in the eighteenth century, when bettors were inspired by pugilism to organize boxing matches. As we've seen, pugilism was part of the Olympic Games in ancient Greece, but didn't appear until the 23rd Olympiad in 688 B.C. The winner of this first contest was Onomastus of Smyrna, who established the first set of boxing rules. Such contests were the exclusive domain of the male nobility of the era. Sometimes fighting in the nude, the contestants wrapped their hands in leather straps that were often weighted with lead balls (*cestus*), thus increasing the impact of the blows and inflicting cruel injuries. Training techniques for pugilism came a long way under the Romans, who invented the protective sandbag and refined the practice of footwork. This was the type of fighting used by gladiators. Banned by those in political and religious power around the start of the eleventh century, boxing fell into obscurity until being rediscovered in the eighteenth century with the arrival of English boxing.

English boxing

English boxing (as opposed to the French or Eastern varieties) first appeared in the eighteenth century. It was organized by bettors who modeled it on pugilism. Because of this (and also because it was a form of dueling that threatened the established social order and the lives of future soldiers, fathers of families, nobles), it was associated with money and with potentially corrupt

VE
ERO

and clandestine practices from the very start. The first boxer recognized as the heavyweight champion was the Englishman James Figg in 1719, but the fights then were still to the death. The first boxing rules were published in 1743 by the Englishman Jack Broughton. Known as the London Prize Ring rules, they defined the area of the ring and established the knockout rule, according to which the contestant who stayed prone on the mat for more than 10 seconds was declared the loser.

In 1857, the *Marquess of Queensberry rules* were drafted under the patronage of the eighth Marquess of Queensberry, who declared boxing the "noble art." These rules were first applied in 1892 and stressed agility rather than force. They prohibited bare-knuckle fighting, hugging, choking, blows to a helpless opponent, and fights to the death. The matches were divided into three-minute rounds with one-minute rest intervals in between. A contestant lost the match when he remained down, either prone or on one knee, for more than 10 seconds. These 1857 rules also stipulated that matches should take place in a 24-foot ring. Consequently, as of the late nineteenth century boxing matches were faster and less violent. Thus, they were able to come out into the open. The last bare-knuckle heavyweight champion was the American John L. Sullivan in 1889. Fighting without gloves (in accordance with the Queensberry rules), Sullivan lost his world championship title on September 7, 1892. The Queensberry Rules continue to govern professional boxing today.

Disenchantment?

The philosophy behind English boxing has been the inspiration for countless novels, films (boxers were the subject of some of the earliest cinematic ventures between 1880 and 1894!), comic books, video games, etc. This sport can turn an ordinary individual into either a champion or a loser. There are countless examples of champions who met with tragic fates. Paradoxically, boxing remains one of the most popular sports because it is open to everyone, regardless of their social situation. This idea caught on quickly in England, the first country to acknowledge individual freedoms, and naturally flourished in the U.S., the "sweet land of liberty."

We know very little about the aristocratic champions. The most famous was Arthur Cravan, born Fabien Avenarius Lloyd (into the family of insurers and lords) and nephew of, among others, Oscar Wilde (the great poet who Queensberry—the same one who defined the rules of the modern ring —brought before the court in an effort to protect his son, who was having "an affair" with Wilde). Cravan devoted his entire life to boxing and poetry. He was responsible for the first modern avant-garde journal (*Maintenant*, 1912) and was considered to be one of the first formulators of the Dadaist movement (1916), but few remember his 1915 encounter with Jack Johnson (1878–1945), the first black boxer to become world champion.

If few boxing champions "finish" well, it must be because boxing teaches them "to destroy a man but never to build a life," as A. Philonenko remarked. This great theoretician of the genre also noted that the number of licensed boxers

The first black boxer, Jack Johnson, 1910

in France dropped from 8,000 in 1950 to around 2,000 in 1980. According to Thierry Gautier, national trainer in English boxing for the French Boxing Federation (FFB), there are currently between 350 and 400 professional boxers in France. Gautier, who attributes this to a "possible disenchantment" with the sport—although it's still very popular—estimates that there around 20,000 boxing fans in France, but distinguishes among several very different practices:

- Boxing as a *leisure activity* in public sports centers;
- Boxing as *educational*, characterized by assault-type competitions taught in physical education courses at universities (competitive or not);
- *Amateur* boxing, practiced in private, neighborhood clubs; and,
- Finally, *professional* boxing.

Gautier assures us that today, future champions are well taken care of, with psychological support, financial safeguards mandated by the government (retirement), and the monitoring of the various vices (drugs, doping, alcohol, betting). For a long time, the concept of ethics found no place in boxing. Today, more than ever, "boxing remains a way for men to edify themselves while gradually internalizing what initially escapes them. Physical strength, self-control, and personal discipline are also part of it. Boxing must become a *paideia*, an education," (Philonenko).

A matter of money?

What seems to fascinate spectators is the idea of the boxing ring as a place of endless possibilities. Even if the men who come together in the ring know each other, especially today when everyone's life is scrutinized by the media and subject to anti-doping tests, they meet on a different footing every time. Nothing is decided in advance, which is where betting comes in. Although betting is as old as the world, it flourished in the twentieth century when it became a veritable industry run by bookmakers. Uncertainly about the outcome of an upcoming match (unless the match is fixed and one of the boxers has been asked to "take a dive") breeds fear. One of the golden rules for boxers, therefore, is not to over think the match.

Some champions have demonstrated a certain reflexive intelligence, including Jack La Motta (*Raging Bull*, the 1980 film by Martin Scorcese, depicts the redemption of an ex-con, his fall, and his rehabilitation by the media), and Marcel Cerdan, who was for a long time the moral boxer for an entire generation (and beyond) and died in a plane crash. Indeed, all the tragic stories of boxers' fates demonstrate that although they all want money and fame, they have an even greater thirst for combat, challenge and superiority, promethean ambitions that cause most of them to self-destruct, and that few manage to escape. Boxing also contains something of the country fair or show that started out in rural areas and moved to the cities. Until the 1960s, matches were accompanied by major publicity campaigns (posters, rebroadcasts on radio and television, busing of supporters, bidding for tickets, and unbeliev-

able spin-off products). Unlike other sports, television did nothing to halt the emptying of boxing arenas. It appears that boxing has gotten a bad reputation from the sometimes enormous sums of money at stake and the supposed ties to the mob, as well as the racism inherent in the fact that boxing lays no ethnic ground rules.

Basic rules

The death of the Cuban boxer Paret in 1962 is often cited as being the result of the worst refereeing to occur since the end of World War II. However, the "third man" who can't be struck has been around for much longer than that. "Without a referee," writes A. Philonnenko, "boxing becomes a fight to the death, which is something human beings would be better off avoiding."

Generally speaking, a referee must evaluate two types of movement:

- *Jabs* ("right cross," "left jab"), *hooks*, *uppercuts*, and *swings* (a beginner's round-arm blow that is too often badly aimed); and

- *Bobbing and weaving*, which is allowing the opponent to swing over your head and facing him again, *side-stepping*, and *slipping*, which is avoiding blows with small movements of the head.

Assuming the "guard position" means preparing to simultaneously anticipate the opponent's blows and throw punches, whence the expression "double détente." During the first minutes of the "Fight of the Century" (meaning one of the greatest matches in the history of modern boxing and, therefore, the last English boxing match of mythic proportions) between Mohammad Ali (formerly Cassius Clay) and George Foreman in Kinshasa, Zaire on October

30, 1974, Ali had his back to the ropes, absorbing and parrying Foreman's powerful blows while the crowd roared. For six rounds, Foreman tired himself out while Ali saved his strength. You know the rest. In the eighth round, Foreman was knocked out by Ali's legendary right. Ali had the inconceivable idea of altering his game and changing the stakes at the last minute. No one could have predicted how the match would end.

Training

Several types of conditioning are required when preparing for a boxing match:

- *Jogging*, which builds wind, calves and thighs, and especially the deconstructed practice of short and long strides in rapid, arrhythmic and prolonged sequences. Contrary to popular belief, however, jogging is necessary only once a week. The value of jogging outdoors is that it's a form of aerobic exercise (a prolonged effort lasting over 40 seconds and requiring oxygen).
- *Shadow boxing*, which means imagining an opponent, visualizing his strategies and offering tactical responses. It's a phase of active mental preparation. Part of preparing for an approaching fight is gathering information on the opponent.
- Complete medical examination and a proper diet.

Kickboxing

Kickboxing is a synthesis of French boxing (savate), full-contact karate and Thai boxing (muay Thai). All three of these disciplines combine foot and fist tech-

Kickboxing is a synthesis of French boxing (savate), full-contact karate and Thai boxing (muay Thai).

niques with English boxing rules (ring, ropes, referee, judges, rounds, pauses, gloves) and are practiced in a ring. These sports are relatively new and their rules are constantly evolving. Federations for international competitions come and go almost daily.

French boxing / savate

Savate French boxing is practiced in a spirit of attack similar to fencing. In the mid-eighteenth century, France had two kicking techniques: *chausson*, which was revered by the Marseille mob scene, and savate, which was practiced in the north. Whereas chausson employs only the feet, savate allows fighters to use their feet and open hands. Savate was mainly practiced by Parisian thugs, such as Michel Chasseux, who established the first rules and opened a training establishment in about 1820 in the infamous La Courtille district of Paris. Michel Lecour, after a burning defeat at the hands of a London boxer in around 1830, carefully studied English boxing techniques, returned to France and combined these rules with the kicks of savate and chausson. He then opened an establishment in Paris, which quickly attracted the celebrities of his day (Alexandre Dumas, Théophile Gautier) and the aristocracy (which has always felt at home with the criminal element).

But the real "father" of French boxing was Joseph Charlemont (born in 1839), who started practicing this sport in 1860 and published his first book on technique in 1877. He taught his method to his son, Charles, who won a celebrated match against an English boxer, Jerry Driscoll, in 1899. At the turn of the century, French boxing flourished. It was taught in the army, in schools,

and at sports clubs. Georges Carpentier (who would later become European champion in English boxing) began his career in 1907 with French boxing. However, French boxing and its amateur spirit was soon abandoned in favor of English boxing and its professional fights. World War I dealt a stunning blow to French boxing with the tragic deaths of its teachers and many practitioners at the front.

Between the World Wars, French boxing was unable to withstand the tidal wave of English boxing. By 1940, no more than 500 French boxers remained. Count Pierre Baruzy tried to revive it after the Liberation (August 1944). In 1965, the National French Boxing Committee was formed. In 1972, the "French Federation of Savate French Boxing and Associated Disciplines" was created, followed by the "Savate French Boxing International Federation" (FIBFS) on March 23, 1985, which has members in eleven countries. The blows are real in competition, but only feigned in training. Matches take place in a ring and generally follow rules similar to those of English boxing. The kicks come from savate and include chassés (piston-like kicks), fouettés (whip kicks), revers fouettés (reverse whip kicks using the sole of the foot), revers balancés (reverse leg swings), etc. Because kicks to the face, torso and legs are permitted, there is also a "chassé figure" (chassé aimed at the face), a "fouetté bas" (whip kick aimed at the legs) or "médian" (whip kick aimed at the torso). The punches are borrowed from English boxing and must land above the belt. The boxers ("tireurs" in French) wear a one-piece suit that covers the legs

Savate French boxing is practiced in a spirit of attack similar to fencing.

and torso, but not the arms. They also wear gloves like those used in English boxing and shoes laced behind the ankle to prevent injury.

Savate French boxing is an exclusively amateur sport with a certain intellectual aspect. It has an educational component, in accordance with the spirit that has long fueled athletic practices in France, which is how it has become embedded in the schools. Despite several attempts to organize international competitions, it's having a hard time adapting itself to the modern concept of sports (big entertainment, financial contributions, promotion by the media).

Savate is most challenging on the technical level. It's characterized by a broader array of kicks. The leg is the weapon most often used (in "groupé-fouetté" position, the knee is raised first and then the leg extended), whereas in other fighting styles, kicks are "thrown," using momentum to increase the effectiveness of the blows.

Full contact karate

Full-contact karate was created in the United States in 1974. It was invented by the fight promoter Mike Anderson in association with taekwondo champion Jhoon Rhee to meet the needs of the film industry, which was looking for a discipline that could compete with the techniques used in Bruce Lee movies. Because many karatekas want to actually land their blows, full-contact has practically replaced karate in the U.S. It was first introduced in France by karate champion Dominique Valéra. The Belgian actor Jean-Claude Van Damme is the ambassador of this sport in films.

American full-contact karate combines punching techniques and the structure of English boxing matches with kicking techniques inspired by karate. Unlike other kickboxing styles, it doesn't allow blows below the belt. And unlike muay Thai, the elbows and knees may not be used. The fighter wears trousers and gloves, with a bare torso. Feet are also bare, but protected by a flexible foam slipper without a sole. Beneath the trousers, fighters wear shin guards. The sport was named "full-contact karate" to designate a type of karate where blows actually made contact with the opponent.

Full-contact karate was extremely successful in France toward the end of the 1980s. It attracted many karatekas for reasons of sport (actual striking of blows), but also for financial reasons, because it can be practiced professionally. In addition, its prohibition of blows below the belt gives it a unique aesthetic. It also benefited from a positive image because it came from America. However, many amateur kickboxers have tended to prefer other disciplines (savate French boxing, kickboxing, and muay Thai) which, from a recreational point of view, offer a wider variety of techniques (particularly the possibility of attacking the legs). Like English boxing, these others allow fighters to stand closer together and demand less agility. In addition, sport karate has itself changed, offering the possibility of landing blows while wearing pads, which has considerably diminished interest in full-contact karate.

Kickboxing

Created in the United States in the early 1960s, kickboxing is a form of boxing that permits all types of kicks above the belt, where the only targets below the belt are round kicks to the thighs and sweeps to the foot. In the U.S., kickboxing is a generic term for sport boxing in which the contestants use kicks and certain martial practices originally from Asia. It's important to note that most martial art schools in the U.S. participate in open kickboxing events as well as promoting their own disciplines.

According to many accounts by American champions, the first competitive matches in the ring and on mats took place in 1962 and combined various styles including karate, taekwondo, kempo, bando, etc. But it wasn't until 1977 that American kickboxing was officially recognized with the establishment of a federation of professional full-contact karate champions who wanted to fight the Asians in a sort of competition that allowed the percussive use of the lower limbs. It would be real boxing, combining both punching techniques (English boxing) and kicks (karate, taekwondo).

In order to differentiate among the different activities both in Europe and in the U.S., a distinction was made between two types of sports: kickboxing, which allows kicking the thighs, and full-contact karate, which does not. Kickboxing arrived in France in the late 1970s, where the first federations were established in the early '80s. Many groups tried to take control of kickboxing, until 1999 when the French Federation of Kickboxing and Associated Disciplines (FKB-DA) was formed, and then approved by the government on May 3, 2000.

The Federation currently has 6000 members, 210 clubs, and 24 leagues, and the numbers are growing by approximately 15 percent every season. Complementary disciplines include light kickboxing, cardio-kickboxing (very popular in fitness clubs in the United States), and kickboxing for self-defense.

Like the other kickboxing styles, matches are held in a ring. The contestants wear gloves and, if desired, foot protection. They strike with both fists and feet. The punches are derived from English boxing. The kicks are identical to those of muay Thai and can be applied to any part of the body (face, torso, and legs). According to those who practice the sport, the uniform is more like that of full-contact karate (trousers and foot protection) than that of muay Thai (shorts and bare feet). Kickboxing is very similar to savate French boxing (same weapons and same authorized targets), which is why it's so easy for some boxers to change over to kickboxing when they decide to go professional. But it's a long way from the spirit of attack that characterizes savate French boxing. Since kickboxing permits kicking the legs, practitioners of this discipline stand closer to their opponents than in full-contact karate. Often, kicks are used only to strike the legs and undermine the opponent's foundation. Punches are used on the torso and head, which makes kickboxing very similar to English boxing.

1
2
4

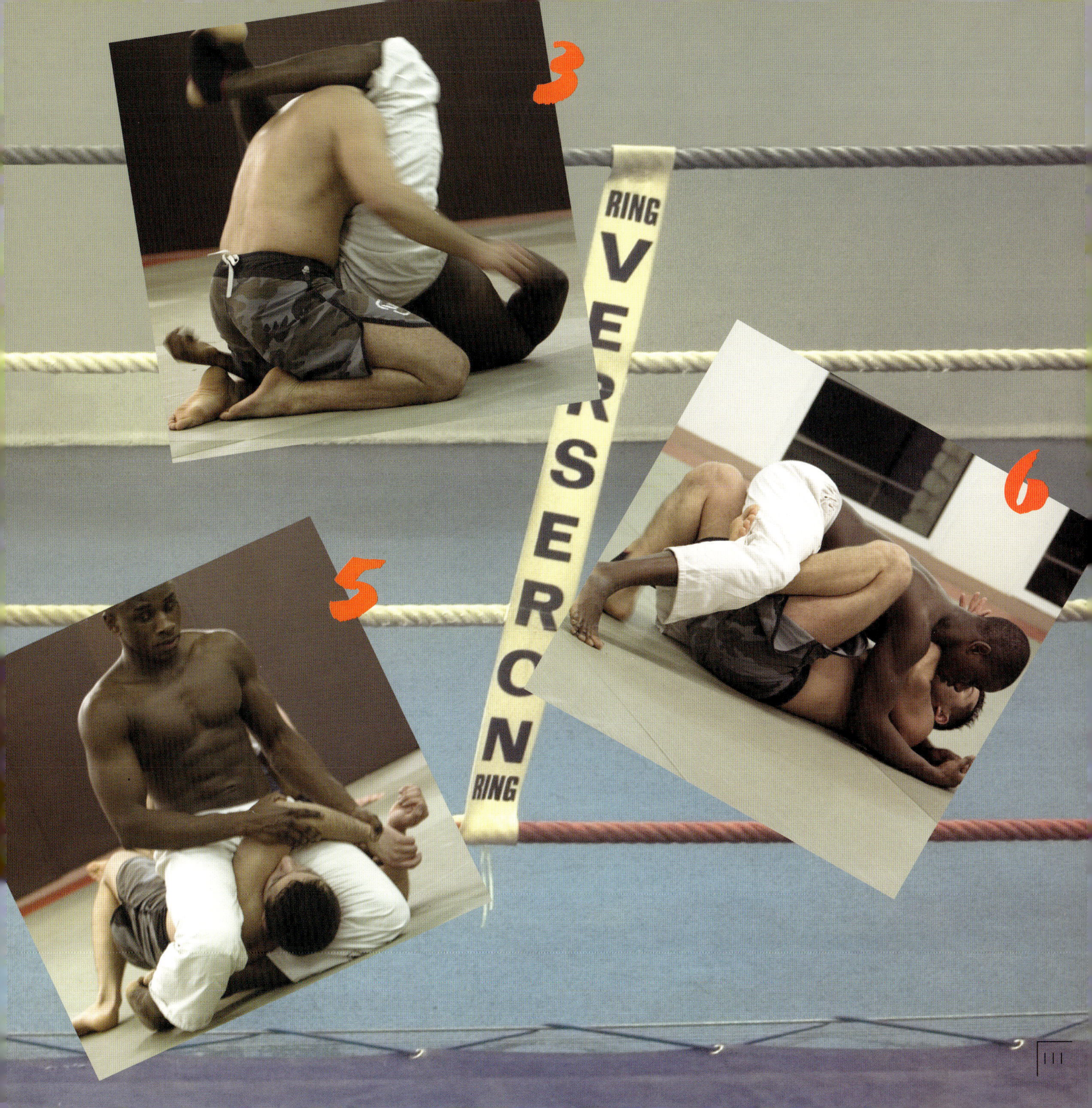
3
5
6
RING
VERSERCN
RING

Muay Thai

Muay Thai, also known as Thai boxing, combines ancient kicking, elbowing, and kneeing techniques similar to karate with the punches of English boxing. It also borrows English boxing's basic rules. In addition to blows to the body, it also permits holding and throwing techniques similar to those in judo. All parts of the body are legal targets (face, torso, and legs). The Thai boxer wears gloves and shorts as in English boxing, while the feet are bare. Muay Thai boxing matches are of uniform length, consisting of five rounds of three minutes each and two-minute pauses in between.

The story goes that many centuries ago, Nai Khanom Dtom, a legendary hero, was captured by the Burmese. In the presence of the king of Burma, Nai fought a dozen adversaries, one at a time, in rapid succession—using his bare hands, of course! As a reward for his courage, the king gave him his freedom. In 1411 at the death of King Sen Muang Ma, his two sons Yi and Fang wanted to seize the throne. Because their two armies failed to defeat one another on the battlefield, they decided to settle their dispute with a duel. Each side chose its best boxer. In the end, Fang's man was beaten and Yi took the throne. The technique used by his "boxer" became a school.

In the sixteenth century, muay Thai was taught in military academies and then spread to the peasants. Contestants protected their fists with cotton bands that they soaked in glue, and then dipped into ground glass! Because of its deadly nature, Thai boxing was banned in 1921. Then in around 1930, it reappeared with rules and punching techniques adopted from English boxing (gloves, ring). As a result of the growth of the tourist trade in Thailand, the West discovered Thai boxing. In Thailand, it's an important rite of passage for the youth. Matches follow a fascinating ritual. Before fighting, the boxers kneel in prayer, and the entire match is conducted with background music played live by a small band of Thai musicians. Of the three kickboxing styles descended from Asian techniques, muay Thai is the oldest. It first spread to Holland and soon began to rival full-contact karate and the "Japanese" version. Using the body's four natural weapons, muay Thai is a very holistic sport. Because a blow can come from anywhere, it requires that fighters be extremely alert. The holds allow "Thai" boxers to catch their breath. As far as throws are concerned, they don't earn any points but, in addition to their psychological impact, are one way to escape from a clinch.

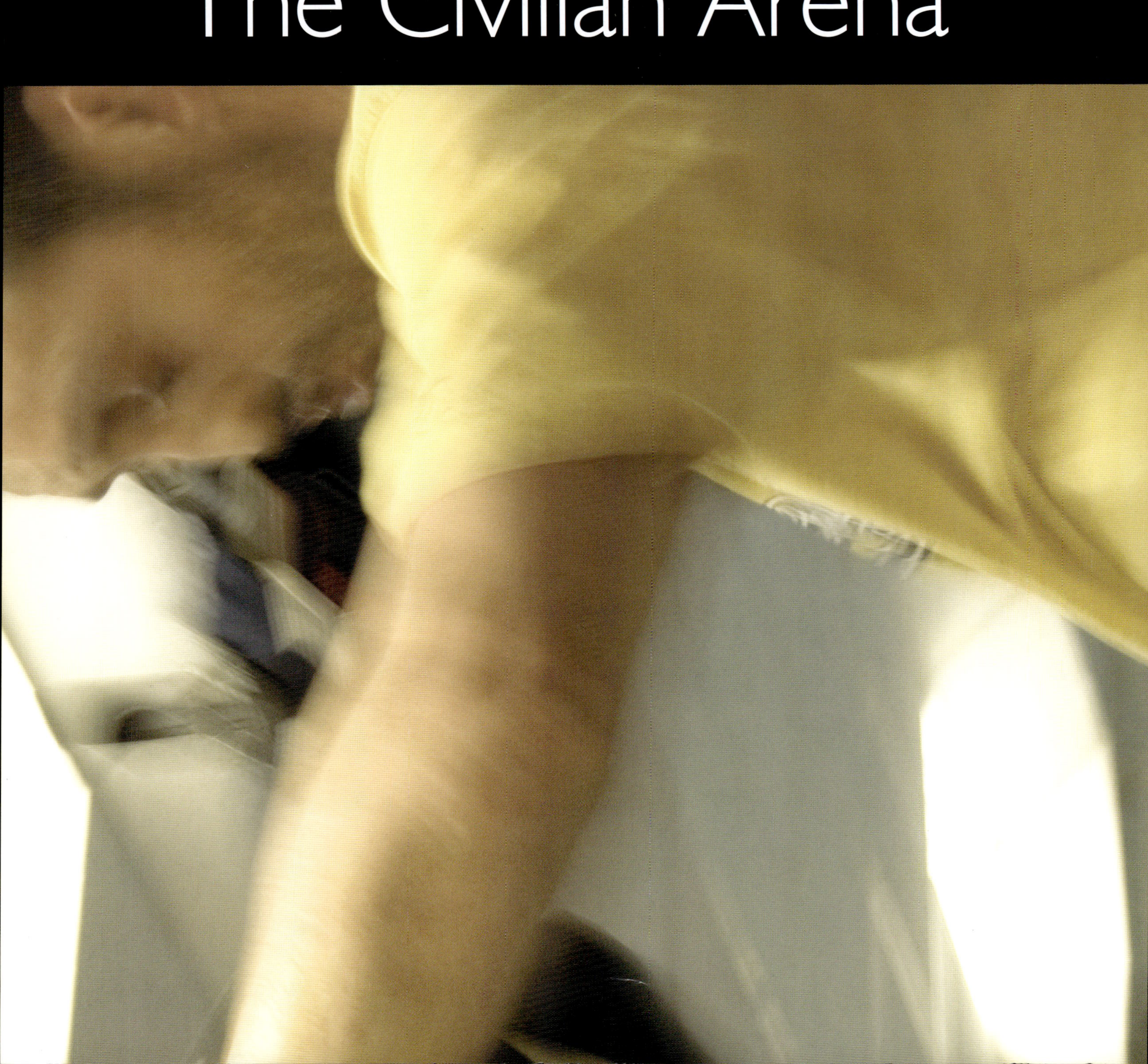

The Civilian Arena

Some see fighting as a leisure activity, hobby, or a necessary expense for preserving their mental health, while others make it their profession. Once the techniques of combat are fully mastered, they can lead to a career that has nothing to do with competition or athletics. Sometimes both activities can be practiced together, but this is rare, given the rigorous schedule required in certain civilian professions.

The fighting professions

Surveillance and security

Should we be worried? Among the fastest-growing professions today are those related to surveillance, civil, personal or building security, bodyguarding, etc. The paradox of a democratic society is that we often have to defend ourselves from the enemies within. Dangers from without are the army's job and the government's responsibility. In addition to the police, who are also under the direct jurisdiction of the state or of a local authority (federal, regional, etc.), there are numerous private companies that offer security services for hire.

Trainers

Professions related to athletic or personal training are also growing rapidly. Some fighting sports might experience a sudden growth in popularity because they're in style (often starting in the U.S.), because of an Olympic or world championship event, or as a result of a cultural event (book, film, video game). The need for trainers is then felt. Other sports have too many trainers. Generally speaking, anyone who wants to pursue a career as a trainer should contact

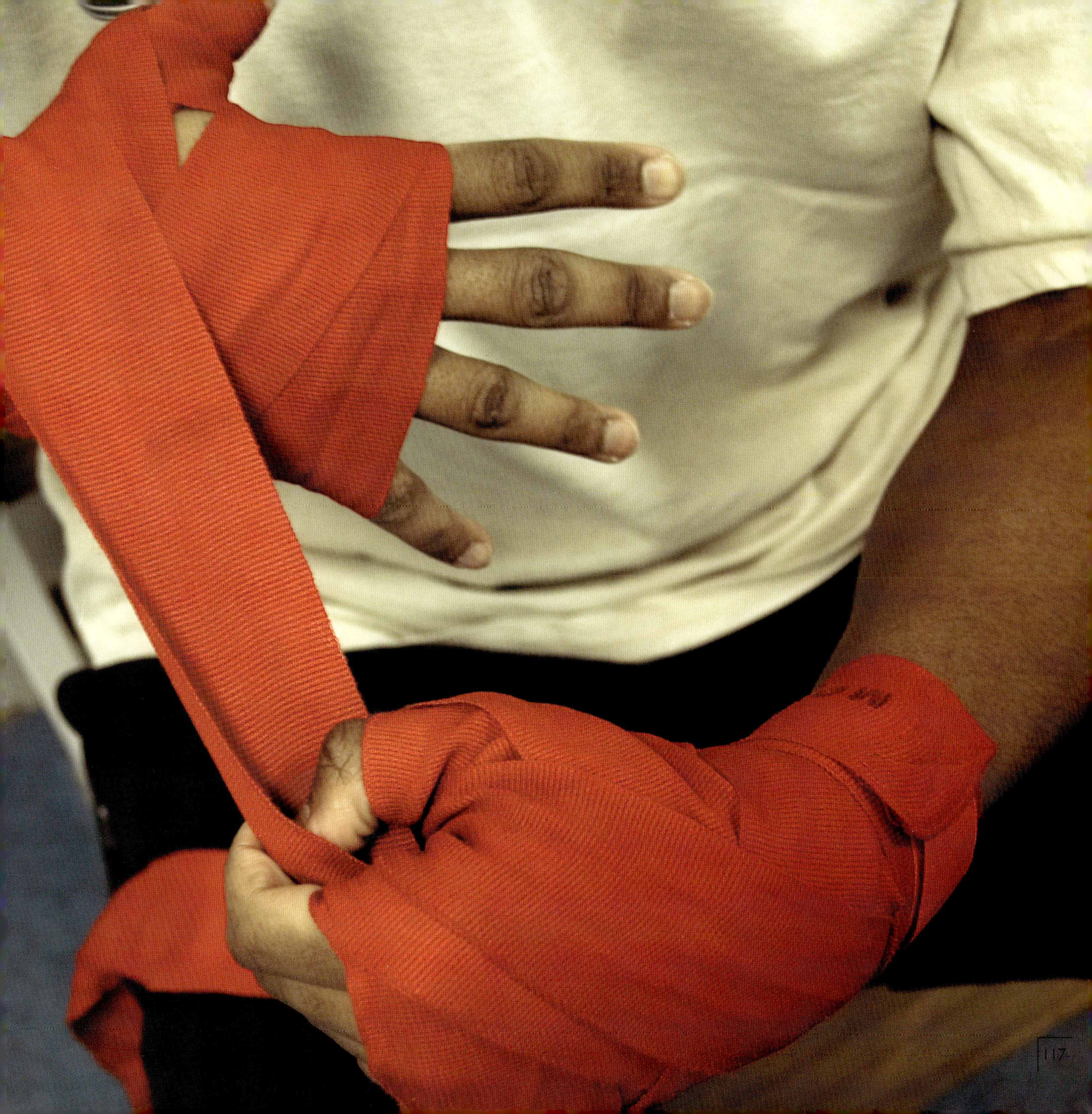

the national and local federations to obtain the necessary information. When a new fighting sport appears ("total combat" or *bugei*, for example), this could be the moment to create a "dojo" with some partners. On the individual level, there are also personal trainers. It's not uncommon to find combat experts who train at home. Although such practices are very expensive, they aren't regulated and could entail both health and financial risks.

Special training

This term refers to training for professions in commando units, the police, army, etc. With the rise of terrorism, these professions have seen significant growth since the early 1990s. A real bodyguard will have gone through this type of training. Specific preparations include the basic principles of close combat, of course, but for the "neutralization on the ground" of risky situations, including:

- Checking persons (identity, personal effects)
- Checking vehicles (cars, truck, airplanes)
- Searching techniques
- Techniques for immobilizing a person even when armed (rifle, club, etc.)
- Techniques for checking a load of animals
- Removing an uncooperative individual
- Investigating unfamiliar places
- Techniques for rescuing people in distress
- Techniques for guarding a person closely or discretely.

Combat in hostile environments such as water, fire, etc., should also be included in this training. None of these techniques is intended to be used to take a life, but are meant to save lives, first the lives of the group, and then of the attacker.

Women fighters

With the advent of gender studies (male, female, transgendered) and "cultural" (non-ethnocentric) studies in the 1980s, no study of fighting would be complete without women's fighting.

A legend?

From the very start, fights between women have been part of a number of legends that include the goddesses Hera and Athena and the mythical Amazons, of course, but also the stories of Atalante or Thetis and Peleus, female Spartan warriors (contemporary witnesses disagree on this), female gladiators, and woman warriors as epitomized by Joan of Arc (but also Al-Kahina). Undoubtedly, they have some basis in truth, but the representations portraying these myths (bas reliefs, vases, painting, epics) can't be considered absolute proof. In the late nineteenth century, ethnologists produced drawings and photographs showing that in certain tribes (Indonesia, Amazon, Pacific Islands), some of the women engage in violent combat. Modern Japan has revealed that the martial arts were not entrusted to men alone. Archeologists have recently uncovered inscriptions on tombs dating back to the Roman occupation of England describ-

It wasn't until the 1960s that women became eligible to compete on the international level.

ing the essedaria, the female gladiators who fought from chariots. The history of woman fighters has yet to be written.

Entertainment

During the mid-nineteenth century, certain "libertine" theaters held performances of battles between female gladiators, involving naked women who simulated the violence of ancient combat. Such "archeological fantasies" attracted large crowds. They're still being performed today in the United States, for example, where there are annual competitions between women disguised as predatory warriors or who wrestle in mud, whipped cream, cake, chocolate syrup, etc. Some find it erotic, others degrading, but this type of fighting is in no way an art. It's purely for entertainment and, it must be said, embodies very male fantasies. Such fantasies emerged in the nineteenth century out of the imaginations of writers such as Leopold von Sacher-Masoch (from whose name the term "masochism" was derived, involving self-flagellation), Bram Stoker (Dracula), and even Octave Mirbeau (shoe fetish), and painters such as Toulouse Lautrec, Cham, and Couturier. Virago, strong woman, dominatrix, succubus, neo-Lilith, vamp, Sapho, all of these are metamorphoses of an image of femininity that still frightens some men (but it's a familiar fear and a turn-on) who regularly frequent strip clubs and brothels.

An athletic reality?

Myths, country fairs, and showbiz apart, since the nineteenth century women have been trying to assert themselves through certain recreational and athletic practices (swords, pistols, wrestling, boxing) despite being marginalized by

RSERON
RING

the men. These societies of women first appeared in England, starting with "prize-fighting" in the streets of London in 1720 when Elizabeth Stokes was referred to as a woman capable of using weapons and fists "as well as a man." In April 1795, the essayist Allen Guttman reported a fight near the New Road in London between Mrs. Mary Ann Fielding and a "Jewess of Wentworth Street," won by the former in 80 minutes. There were 70 knockdowns and a purse of 11 guineas (10,000 Euros by today's standards). Beginning in 1768, the famous James Figg began inviting women to fight in his *Amphitheatre*, a sort of early boxing ring that was like a music hall. All these fights were, of course, more or less illegal. Until 1968 (in Europe, at least), the woman's place was still very much "in the home."

At the start of the nineteenth century, this form of entertainment became extremely popular and matches between female boxers were organized. The boxers wore gloves to prevent damage to their faces (whereas a scar on a man is considered manly!). At this point in time, class relations in London were evolving. The Irish fought the English in the streets and laborers fought the bourgeoisie or aristocrats (who were fascinated by violent or ritualistic street practices such as boxing, tattoos, prostitution).

In the mid-nineteenth century, the first scientists to test endurance included women in their study and discovered, to their utter amazement, women's unsuspected capacity for wrestling, boxing. At the end of the nineteenth century, when the first "scandalous" feminists, suffragettes appeared in Berlin, Paris, New York, and London, real boxing matches were organized between women, but remained underground or were held as "follies" in places such as the Moulin Rouge, as described by the writer Francis Carco in *Jésus la Caille* (1914), or at circuses or fairs. In 1898, when Thomas Edison succeeded in filming the famous *Gordon Sisters* (the first women to win the title of "Champion Lady Bag Punchers"), they were just an act.

From 1920 to 1930, fights between women progressed from vaudeville to circuses, cabarets, gymnasiums, athletic clubs and, finally, to the professional level. The country that made it all possible was the U.S. Competitions were organized to find "the strongest woman in the world," along with fights between men and women, and weightlifting or sledgehammer competitions. The American Ada Ash (1906-2004) was able to lift a platform with a horse on it! But the real champion was Ruby Allen (66 kilograms, born in Saint Louis, Missouri), who taught herself how to box and then conquered wrestling in the 1930s, winning 70 matches against anyone who cared to challenge her, since there was not yet an official women's federation. It wasn't until the 1960s that women became eligible to compete on the international level.

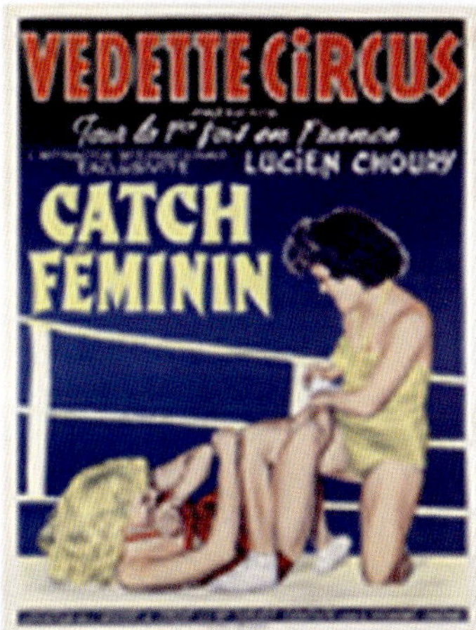

First poster of Female wrestling in France, Paris 1953

He was so successful that in 1948, a statue of Joe Palooka was erected in Indiana, his supposed home state.

(above) Folies Bergeres cabaret poster,
Paris 1900

(right) Joe Palooka, 1940 by Ham Fischer

Leisure

The myth of the total fight

A recent myth in modern Western culture and in the male imagination, among other places, is that of the "total fight" as depicted in *Fight Club*, both the novel by Chuck Palahniuk and the film (David Fischer, 1999). The premise of the story is that, as highly socialized, policed, controlled and uniform beings, we all need to "explode" (to find ourselves?) and fight without restrictions. One punch and a person is dead. Some fables (since that's what most of them are) focus on our lack of individuality and the fact that modern Western societies tend to destroy our humanity, which also includes our natural affinity for violence, blood, hand-to-hand combat—in other words, for fighting and for death. We think we're immortal because advertising tells us we are, according to Brad Pitt in Fischer's movie. The story is that in New York, the movers and shakers of Wall Street unwind after work by fighting in secret rooms in the basements of their financial institutions. But people say a lot of things! The only thing we know for sure is that people will never stop exploring (and relearning) the limits of their own bodies.

Comic books

The fights and altercations in comic books, peppered as they are with interjections (biff, bam, splat) and portraying young heroes or superheroes (including heroines like Wonder Woman) are an undeniable source of imaginary combat, and not just for kids. Comics about fighting appeared in the U.S. in the 1920s as an offshoot of pulp fiction, which was first issued to doughboys in World

NOW GO OUT AN' LET
'IM HAVE IT RIGHT IN
TH' STUMMICK!!

War I in 1917. But comics were also influenced by popular romances of the late eighteenth century, and they're distant cousins of the tales of chivalry and defenders of the poor, the widow, and the orphan. The most likeable of these has to be Joe Palooka, the fair-haired tough guy who was extremely popular after the Crash in 1929. Created by Ham Fisher in 1928, he starts as a 15-year-old boy from a poor, immigrant background who becomes a boxing champion. He was so successful that in 1948, a statue of Joe Palooka was erected in Indiana, his supposed home state. The director Reginald Le Borg filmed the adventures of Joe Palooka (1946–1961), starring Joe Kirkwood.

Video games

It goes without saying that the flourishing international video game industry would be nothing without fight simulation software (armies or kickboxing). Games such as *Street Fighter* (urban brawls where you fight on the side of the law), *Dragon Ball*, and *Doom* have been highly successful. But although the joystick might keep your fingers nimble, it doesn't give you flexible limbs or a balanced emotional life. Video games are good for unwinding, but are no substitute for real combat or physical sports.

(left) Captain America, 1941,
Joe Simon & Jack Kirby
(right) Popeye the Sailor, 1929,
Elzie Crisler Segar

Part Five:
Appendix

Books: Selective bibliography

Ardant du Picq, Charles: *Studies on Combat*

Caillois, Roger: *Man and the Sacred*

Fanon, Frantz: *Black Skin, White Masks*

Fisher, Ham: *Joe Palooka*, Harvey (comics, 1928–1961)

Fox, James A.: *Boxing*

Frazer, J. G.: *The Worship of Nature*

Gardner, Leonard, *Fat City*, 1967

Grecco, Lawrence: *Turkish Wrestling*, Apollon Press, 2004

Guttman, Allen: *Women's Sports: A History*, Columbia University Press, 1991

Hemingway, Ernest: *The Battler*

Lawrence, D. H.: *Women in Love* (Chapter XX "Gladiatorial")

Léal, Frédéric: *Let's go*, roman, POL, 2005

London, Jack: *The Game*

Mailer, Norman: *Fight of the Century*

Orwell, George: *Down and Out in Paris and London*

Toole, F. X.: *Million Dollar Baby: Stories from the Corner*

Wacquant, Loïc: *Body and Soul: Notebooks of an Apprentice Boxer*

Films

Boxing: Selective filmography

Pioneers:

Michael Leonard vs. Jack Cushing, Thomas Edison, 1894

The Boxing Kangaroo, Birt Acres, 1896

Boxing for Points, Veriscope Company, 1897 (documentary)

Silent films:

The Knockout, Charlie Chaplin, 1914

The Champion, Charlie Chaplin, 1915

Battling Butler, Buster Keaton, 1926

Black-and-white:

The Champ, King Vidor, 1931

Any Old Port, Laurel & Hardy, 1932

The Prizefighter and the Lady, W.S. Van Dyke, 1933

The Milky Way, Harold Lloyd, 1935

Kid Galahad, Michael Curtiz, 1937

The Idol, Alexandre Esway, 1947

The Set-Up, Robert Wise, 1949

Champion, Mark Robson, 1949

Alias The Champ, Gorgeous George, 1950

Somebody up There Likes Me, Robert Wise, 1956

The Harder They Fall, Mark Robson, 1956

Killer's Kiss, Stanley Kubrick, 1955

Requiem for a Heavyweight, Ralph Nelson, 1962

Color, United States:

Golden Gloves, Canada, 1961 (documentary)

Fat City, John Huston, 1972

Rocky, John Avildsen, 1976

Raging Bull, Martin Scorcese, 1980

Tough Enough, Richard Fleisheir, 1983

Homeboy, Michael Seresin, 1988

Diggstown, Michael Ritchie, 1992

Le Montreur de boxe, Dominique Ladoge, 1995

The Great White Hype, Reginald Hudlin, 1996

When We Were Kings, Leon Gast, 1996

Snatch, Guy Ritchie, 2000

Hurricane Carter, Norman Jewison, 2000

A Fighter Blues, Daniel Lee, 2000

Girl Fight, Karyn Kusama, 2000

Ali, Michael Mann, 2002

Billie Elliot, Stephen Daldry, 2003

The Boxer, Jim Sheridan, 2003

Million Dollar Baby, Clint Eastwood, 2004

Cinderella Man, Ron Howard, 2005

Appendix

Color, France:

Edith et Marcel, Claude Lelouch, 1981

Fureur, Karim Dridi, 2003

Poids léger, Jean-Pierre Améris, 2004

Casablanca Driver, Maurice Barthélémy, 2004

Chock Dee (Dida), Xavier Durringer, 2004

Noble Art, P. & S Deux, 2005 (documentary about Pascal Bénichou)

Virgil, Mabrouk el Mechri, 2005

Frappes interdites, Bernard Malaterre, 2005

Wrestling, kickboxing, etc.: selective filmography

Spartacus, Stanley Kubrick, 1958

Duelists, Ridley Scott, 1977 (adapted from Joseph Conrad)

Paradise Alley, Sylvester Stallone, 1978

Grunt The Wrestling Movie, Allan Holzman, 1985

Far & Away, Ron Howard, 1992

Only The Strong, Sheldon Lettich, 1993

The Quest, Jean-Claude Van Damme, 1996

Fight Club, David Fincher, 1999

Gladiator, Ridley Scott, 2000

City of God, Fernando Meirelles, 2002

Gangs of New York, Martin Scorcese, 2003

Danny The Dog, Louis Letterrier, 2004

Reversal, Alan Vint, 2005

Scorpion, Julien Seri, 2006

Websites

International Federation of Associated Wrestling Styles

http://www.fila-wrestling.com

Fédération Française de Lutte

http://www.fflutte.com

The Bashpelivanns of Turkey

http://www.bashpelivanns.com

World Wrestling Entertainment

http://www.wwe.com

Sumo

http://www.chez.com

Mexican Wrestling

http://www.mexique-fr.com

French Federation of SAVATE French Boxing

http://www.ffsavate.com

Recommended Visual Art (besides photos by Ph. Vaurès)

- Gilgamesh Cylinder Seal (Louvre)

- *Pugilists*, painted fresco from the Palace of Knossos, Crete,—1400 A.D.

- Michelangelo: *Two Men Wrestling*, chiaroscuro in the Louvre, Paris + various engravings deposited at the Louvre, cf. Pascal Torrès

- Antonio Pollaiuolo (Florence circa 1432–Rome circa 1498) *The Battle of the Nudes*, Musée du Louvre, Département des arts graphiques, Collection Edmond de Rothschild, 6813 L.R

- Photographs from the late 19th century, e.g. Muybridge (motion studies)

- Rodolphe Julian. 1879. Grand in-8, VI-387 pp. and 17 woodcuts h.t. Famous work constituting the apex of homoerotic iconography. (1839–1907)

- Poster of the Folies Bergères by Charles Lévy, 1888: "Grandes luttes, troupe Pietro" (Bibliothèque Forney, Paris)

- Jack Johnson, 1910, the first black boxer

- Philippe Perrin, *Mon dernier combat*, Galerie Air de Paris, Nice, 1990

- Wrestling and boxing magazines from 1920–1970

- Comic books (Marvel Comics, etc.)

Appendix

SPECIAL THANKS TO

Bertrand Amoussou, and his students at "La Cite Universitaire de Paris",
   Serge Boutari and Djeylani Dibaga.

Kamel Charef, and his students at the gym of Villeneuve-la-Garenne,
   Mohamed Boukadda, Tarek Mouhoud and Mourad Sari.

Pascal Torres, Curator at the Louvre museum, Paris.

Philippe Vaurès-Santamaria.

Ariel Wizman.